# HARMONZING LIFE AND MIND

# HARMONZING LIFE AND MIND

Dr Somnath Banerjee

ZORBA BOOKS

# ZORBA BOOKS

Published in India by Zorba Books, 2017

Website: www.zorbabooks.com
Email: info@zorbabooks.com

Copyright © Dr Somnath Banerjee

ISBN Print Book - 978-93-86407-91-7
ISBN eBook - 978-93-86407-92-4

Zorba Books Pvt. Ltd.(opc)
Gurgaon, INDIA

Printed at Repro Knowledgecast Limited, Thane

I dedicate this book to my sister Bithika
for her selfless service

# INTRODUCTION

Harmonizing is essential if we want to live our life gracefully. While physical harmonizing will support our body, Harmonizing our mind with our life is the key. How can we tell when our mind and life are not harmonized. We will feel it as resistance physically, mentally, emotionally, spiritually and/or energetically. The cause of all the miseries we have in the world is that men foolishly think pleasure to be the ideal to strive for. We are responsible for what we are; and whatever we wish ourselves to be, we have the power to make ourselves. If,what we are now, has been the result of our own past actions, it certainly follows that whatever we wish to be in future can be produced by our present actions. Buddha is the only prophet who said, "I do not care to know your various theories about God. What is the use of discussing all the subtle doctrines about the soul? Do good and be good. And this will take you to freedom and to whatever truth there is."

The investigation and analysis consists of five books. First book deals with understanding God and truth, Second book contain analysis of Arjuna's question on self development (hamonizung mind and life).. Third book attributes and functionalities of life are highlighted, fourth book deals with functioning of mind and lastly random results of harmonized life and mind ,Some of the comments of masters and seekers of Speaking tree are included for your information at the end of each book.

My earlier books Introspection published by Auther House (UK) and other Results of consciousness published by Zorba Publication India deal mostly with own life and consciousness. Present aim is to harmonise the experiences and present you with harmonized life.

Dr S S Banerjee

# INDEX

BOOK 1.

UNDERSTAND, GOD AND TRUTH

# BOOK 1. UNDERSTAND GOD AND TRUTH

## COMMENTS

# 1. UNDERSTAND

Between the grinding stones, ground and sky,
where is the time to understand or be understood..
Everyday - a frenzied effort for survival
or to maintain status quo, but alas
moving finger of time writes a different script
which is not obliterated even if you try to.

Yet without understanding
you can not progress
in any domain of your activity
 be it physical, mental or spiritual.
Most tragedies occur due to misunderstanding.
 Yet it very difficult to make someone understand.
Scriptures of all religion are in parables
 you cannot understand them without a master.
One teacher had remarked
'there are so many things you don't understand, so what, leave it',
' but sir, I want to understand' 'well that is your problem'
And then 'come to my chamber and we will discuss'.
There are so many things about *life*
 that you don't understand,
you can remain ignorant and be happy about it.
But nature makes you understand,
it is quite painful you may complain
that nobody understand you.
All hypocrisy and diplomacy are trivial
 and mundane in life's journey.
You have to understand

*Comments attached*

# 2. UNDERSTAND IMMORTALITY OF LIFE,

Growth is fundamental characteristic of life function. you acquire a childhood body, A youth body, and an old age body during this life, and you acquires another body after death. The singularity at the bound state of birth and death entails life function is not defined. Some effervescent state of life function exist which after regeneration i.e. amplified, reshaped and retimed is ready for interaction. The evolved life function is ready for reproduction under congenial ambient condition

The concept of hell and heaven after death is bullshit. The contacts of the senses with the sense objects give rise to the feelings of heat and cold, pain and pleasure. The feelings are confined in the mind, software for functioning of human brain. When body perishes these feeling also perishes, There is nothing good or bad for life function, they make their presence felt after embodiment. Death is certain for the one who is born, and birth is certain for the one who dies. This is essential for immortality of life

## 3. KNOW YOUR BEING

In the duality of Love-Hate
Nothing fails like success,
So know your own being
Only that satisfies, never fails.
Increase your knowledge
Let others look up to you
But know your own being
Success is not all your own.

You be instrument for the occasion
Choose the appropriate mission
Be firmly instrumental
To spread everlasting happiness
More you serve others
Regardless of personal welfare
Your returns may not be visible
You shall know your own being.
I wish you the bliss that shall entail
When you know your own being.

*Comments attached*

# 4. PROCESS THAT I SEEK.

Many can say "how" a thing works
Few can explain 'why' it is so,
Anything left to itself, my dear
Goes from orderliness to disorderliness
Very soon they disintegrate into elements
Prognosis of its decay is well documented.
This is the fate of all manifested entity
Only variation is the time to decay'
All that is born shall surely die
All that die is not born again.
Nature is great in its creativity
Hides all its synthesis activity
We all see plant growing from seed
But how seeds are synthesized is hidden
Hidden in the cocoon is beautiful butterfly
So everything that nature conjures up
Is taken up as mystery of the God.
 I have wasted my life in knowing 'why'
This is madness, I know but I do not sigh.
All secret revealed is domain specific
Only invariant is the Process that I seek.

# 5. DEFINATION OF GOD (QUANTUM PHYSICS)

In quantum mechanics Eigen functions pervades all space and time. Its expectation value at any point and time can be measured which vary with ambient condition.. GOD is defined as Absolute reality which is eternal and omnipresent, which is beyond interpretation and beyond comprehension by minds without infinite vision. It is the algorithm of nature for its synthesis and dissolution. It resembles the eigen function operating on multiple Hamiltonian. World together with all its entities is observed by the senses, which changes, and depends on "other" for its state or condition, it involves duality. It can be analyzed and interpreted like the expectation value.,

Some of us seek it as friend

Some of us seek it as loving mate

Some of us seek as mother

Some of us seek it like servant

Some adore it as loving father

Some respect it as fearful almighty

Some worship as formless one

Some possess it like personal deity

Some call him God, the father

Some call him Allah, almighty

Some call him Bhagwan, omnipresent

Some call him Shri Akal, timeless.

*Comments attached*

# 6. ALL MY DOING AND UNDOING IT IS ALL HIS GAME.

Mother said "Krishna is in your heart
Shall respond when you seek help
He shall come to you in different form
Guide you to destiny you may not know.'

Lanky boy being bullied by school bully
Small petty classmate takes him on
He quickly beats retreat, that is it.
I knew that it was Krishna on the Job.

Chosen to take part in elocution competition
I prepared well but lacked confidence
When awarded first prize by Rotary club
I knew it was not me but You on the stage.

Engrossed in research forgot dinner.
A colleague came up with food that night
' how did you know I had no dinner' I enquired
He just smiled, I knew it was Krishna's job.

Having done no physical training I was overweight
Service selection board tests were very intricate
Surprise of surprise I was the only one selected
'why me' it is your destiny, Krishna reminded.

A meta physicist knows heart is that part of brain
That controls the heart, Krishna is in my brain
Whether in Pineal or Pre-fontal cortext, I know not
All my doing and undoing, it is all His game.

# 7. TRANSCENDING TO GODHOOD

The path of becoming God is through four levels of divinity that exists in one's own body

1. Unmanifest Chaitanya,
2. Manifest Chaitanya-Shakti,
3. Consciousness of the manifest chaitanya-shakti in Prana
4. the Individual consciousness (Jeevatma/Mind).

Anybody in theworld, irrespective of caste, creed, merit, nationality, etc., can transcend and become God by being in union with prana. Only ensure :

- Don't rob,
- Don't kill,
- Never ever lie
- Don't get angry,
- Don't think negative about others
- Don't self describe,
- Don't tease others

This is the way of self respect, this is the way to get respected by the world.This is the way of impressing my Lord.

# 8. WHEN MAN CREATED GOD

When man created God, he could blame everything on him. It was his game, he is the player, he is the referee and he is the field. Everything becomes his and mankind are only instrumental for the occasion. Do not mistake him for nature and he is not bound by natures rule. What is he, we do not know. He is ultimate to everything. This ultimate is not defined in absolute terms.

He is only absolute in relative world. He is all and all is his. He is graceful, merciful, full beautiful and full of glory. These attributes do not define him fully. Human intelligence can not perceive him, but he exists we all know and realize or else how can you explain he is beyond human consumption. Your eyes are open but you may not see. Sound near your ear you may not hear. Pinch in your tummy you may ignore. Every reception from senses are processed by mind. Your cognization and perception depends on mind. Mind creates virtual image, so the world you visualize is virtual. It is nothing but illusion of your mind, then is mind God? When mind ceases all action ceases, you are blind, deaf and mute, if you then transcend the physical and mental domain you realize bliss, you are in spiritual domain. You realize God.

Now scientist have created humanoid with artificial intelligence. It is postulated that this multifunctional and multitasking robot may possess intelligence indistinguishable from human intelligence if its dimensional interaction is raised to eleventh order. This clearly indicate that nature can evolve to human intelligence and no God is required for creation. A ninth dimension black hole is in the centre of our galaxy, how that came about is still mystery. Till then God is all in one and one in all

*Comments attached*

# 9. EXISTENCE AS TRUTH

Existence you cannot deny, is truth. How it came about what is the future may be debatable but it looses significance as changes in the existence is neglible. The present evolved state of affair with sun, moon, stars, forces of nature in real and abstract domain look immortal and unchanging thereby may be defined as truth.

Interaction of forces of nature conjured the life element. Multiple diversity of life evolved resulting in human with intelligence and free will. Existence of life is truth.

It is a small world where you exist, beyond which it is rest of the world. The peripheral world do not affect you, Your contribution to it is also minimal. Truth manifests in your world as Pain and pleasure, heat and cold, Highly esteemed and lowly held, Success and failure, attraction and aversion, Good and wicked, friend and foe, Saint and sinner, high and low. Here and hereafter, merits and demerits, real and false. Since existence is polar, every entity is polarized. Also are knowledge and ignorance, Honor and dishonor, Abandonment and envelopment, Protection and destruction, Virtues and vices are true. Your consciousness, unconsciousness and super consciousness are truth. All modes of nature are truth. All life functions are truth. All interaction of life on life are truth.

Your world is full of camouflage, concealment and deceptions. they hide the truth. They take advantage of the limitation of human senses. They may have values in social atmosphere. The naked truth is hidden by wearing masks. All rumors, misinformation, disinformation, tactics and strategies create make believe situations but are false

## 10. INVARIANT OF THE PROCESS
##    YOU COGNIZE AS TRUTH


With all the calculations and computation you have captured
Nothing helps you in deciphering the nature's true equation.
With all the mechanics, classical, quantum and quantum dynamics
Creation of chaos and synthesis by nature refuses prediction.

Fathoming the truth of Sun you go blind
Working in noisy environment you go deaf
Tasting pungent food your taste buds deplete
In putrid location your nose smell no more.

You are amazed by rejecting power of your mind
mind paints different hues, truth you cannot find.
All the organs of perception and action endowed
Peak, plateau and ebbs in performance with time.

Everything looks true when you are at it,
They were illusion of mind when you realize it
Chaos and synthesis in nature go hand in hand
The invariant of the process you cognize as truth.

' As in human body so is the cosmic body
As is in the atom so is in the universe'
Who can deny this wisdom of the Upanishad
Today science has verified this dynamic truth.
The human body is born, grows and then decays and die,
A star is born, becomes giant, then turns dwarf and die,
The atoms consists of central nucleus with revolving electrons
The universe consists of a star with revolving planets.

# 11. BRAHM SATYA JAGAT MITHYA ?

Yes, what is not there but appears is fake or otherwise Illusion. To claim that something is a truth is to claim that it is a determinate matter. To claim that something is a determinate matter is concurrently to claim that it is concurrently impossible for alternatives to be true. To claim that something is true is to deny the truth of alternatives. It is only in indeterminate conditions that alternative possibilities are possible, but, so long as there is indeterminateness, none of the alternative possibilities by themselves are true (or truths). Determinateness is a characteristic necessary for truth. The Universe presents dualities in each entity, multiple probabilities are the rules. Life is a stochastic process everything is changing with time. Universe therefore is false.Lord Krishna's words in Bagawad Gita & Science are matching. In wave particle duality any particle in form can change itself into energy wave on its own under the instigation of Universal Intelligence. Whatever we see is only energy and that energy can manifest into any form. Whatever we see is not there now at the time of seeing. So entire things we see are only fake or Illusion. The reality is Energy the omnipotent GOD or Brahm.

It is important to note that *possibility* and *contingency* as well as *possibly* and *contingently* are not identical or interchangeable pairs of terms, despite the fact that many discussions in modal logic or possible worlds terms might make it seem that these words are necessarily identical and interchangeable. it is incoherent to claim that something is both true and possibly true; however, there is no such incoherence when something is claimed to be both true and contingent or contingently true.

Brahm has not been defined as yet, I shall not attempt it. but In all illusion of the universe there is an invariant law that does not change. That is truth.Which is same in human body as well as cosmic body, which is same in atom as it is in universe(Upanishad).

*Comments attached*

## 12. TRUTH IS THE BIGGEST FORCE

my mother told me that Truth was biggest force and narrated the following story

Once there was a king. He was a strong spiritualist, a dharmik. (upholder of truth.) Whatever he said he did and whatever he did he said. One day the king declared that he would buy anything that remained unsold in the village market. People flocked to the market.

A sculptor brought an idol of the goddess Alakshmi, which negates wealth. Who would want to keep an idol of Alakshmi in their house? Nobody bought it. In the evening the sculptor came to the king and said: "Please take this idol and be true to your words." The king bought it. Alakshmi entered the palace. At midnight the king heard a woman weeping. He approached her, asking, "Mother, why are you weeping? What is the matter?" "I am the goddess of wealth, Rajyalakshmi," she replied. "Now that Alakshmi has entered the palace, how can i live here?" The king said, "Very well, for the protection of Truth i have to keep Alakshmi here. If you do not want to live here, you may go." So the goddess of wealth left.

After some time the Raja heard the sound of footsteps. He saw a man and asked, "Who are you?" The reply was: "I am Narayana." The king asked: "Where are you going?" Narayana replied: "Lakshmi has left the palace, so i shall not live here." The king said, "To protect Truth, i have to keep Alakshmi, and so if you want to leave the palace, you may go; what can i do?" Narayana left. After that all the gods and goddesses left the palace. The king said, "If you all so desire you may go." In the end a glorious personality appeared. "Who are you?" asked the king. The reply was "I am Truth. As all the other gods and goddesses have left the palace, i am also leaving." The king replied, "It cannot be. To protect Truth i kept Alakshmi. how can you leave me?" Truth said, "You are right. I will not leave."

Since Truth remained there, Narayana slowly entered through the back door. The king said to him, "If you wish you may come." Lakshmi followed him, covering her face, because she did not dare to show her face to the king. Then all the gods and goddesses started entering. They said, "Where there is Truth, where there is Narayana and Lakshmi, we shall also be there."

Truth is the biggest force. For those who have such a force, the worldly force is meaningless. You were with Truth, you are with Truth and you will be with Truth. Don't fear anybody. We should move on the path of Truth even if Lakshmi leaves..

# 13. ALL LOGIC.EMOTION AND ACTION ARE TRUE

life is manifestation of life functions beginning in birth and terminating in death. Life interacts with energy system of the brain and consciousness begins to take shape. Your space and time starts now.Your senses starts interacting with external world. Your inner world endowed in the brain complexes - mind, intellect and ego are working overtime to adjust to new environment.

Environment comprises sense objects, your senses are gratified with them and you develop attachment. It can be attractive or repulsive. This attachment is central to interaction of consciousness. All your action and emotion are due to this attachment. There is no pain or pleasure once you are detached. You still bleed when you get cut but pain is below threshold of withstanding it.

From attachment springs desire. two things can happen

1.  Desire fulfilled may be after some striving – you get peace.
2.  Desire not fulfilled – results in anger, desire still persists then it is infatuation. In infatuation there is confusion of memory, loss of reason and leads to your ruin.

All logic, emotions and action are real when you are at it and appears delusion when you are out of it. In electricity we learn about two types of current- one DC direct current and the other AC alternating current. Example of AC current is power supply from Power station whereas example of DC is Battery in mobile car etc. in DC voltage associated with current does not change with time or load whereas in AC voltage varies from positive crest to negative trough. An electric pulse is mixture of AC and DC and exist for small length of time.

Why am I talking about electric pulses?

The electro- chemical reaction in nervous system or neural network give rise to an electric pulse which is trartnsported to brain. The mentro- nervo waves or thought is generated by these pulses. Under guidance of cortex various brain complexes take part and these are time integrated or rejected resulting in logic emotion and action.

Since AC at any instant is DC. All logic, emotion and action are not time invariant and are considered illusion or delusion they are all real at that phase of time.

Every human life perishes but life is immortal so life is truth. So are its ingredient, Female form in the west is considered truth and phallic symbol in the east is considered truth.

*Comments attached*

# 14. BEING CUSTODIAN DON'T ACT LIKE OWNER

Your wealth you may sacrifice
Your women you may sacrifice
Your daily wine you may sacrifice
But these are not your own
Then how can it affect you?
How can it bring peaceful bliss?
Multitude may look at you in awe
Being custodian don't act like owner.

You may struggle as long as you want
You may build mansions as long as you want
Be lost in meditation as long as you want
You are boosting your ego-propagating
You may withstand pain to purify yourself
Pain is only physical and mental perception
With time and medicine it diminishes
Like pleasure you can relinquish pain.
 End of envy lead to change in the object of envy
When you sweat out to outrun the object of envy
Your strivings lead to higher object to envy
Only contentment can decrease upward mobility.
Revenge for loss of honor rages indefinitely
By the time you take revenge the object changes
Only ends when you are incapable or not inclined
End of revenge makes you magnanimous and sane

Fulfillment of need is a pleasant delusion
Need tend to increase with each fulfillment
While life is always decreasing function of time
You may whine or chime but lost in grime
When you are in spiritual domain
Your normal daily routine remain same
You are otherwise numb but your eyes shine
You are at peace and happy condition.

*Comments attached*

# 15. DON'T BELIEVE WHAT YOU SEE

'Don't believe what you see, don't believe what you hear',

Maj Bisham Singh boomed while teaching Camouflage and concealment to the Gentleman cadets. "sir, then what should you believe in?' He glared at us and said 'Gut feeling ' Now what do you see in front of you' ' look in front at a distance of 700m a lone hut, line joining hut and center of the class is general line of direction, at nine o'clock, distance 500m a debris of stone, at 1oo'clock 400m a bunch of bushes, at 1 o'clock 500m a lone tree, at 2o'clock 300m bunch of trees ….

'Look carefully, you will see what you want to see, look through the bushes.' We could see nothing concrete. Then after sometime Maj signaled the demo troop to reveal themselves, they were more than 50 soldiers with guns and rifles.

Though person believe only by direct perception or inferred perception as per Patanjali, the nature is full of delusion with camouflage and concealment. the truth lies hidden. Nature provides multidimensional interaction with multiple hidden layers with their interaction coefficient depending on ambient condition and cosmic mutation. I find that

All laws of physics are range bound equation
All chemical reactions depend on ambient condition
All mathematical treatise are based on approximation
All outcomes are beyond senses and its perception.

A person traversing the spiritual domain in search of truth must transcend the senses and modes of nature. He has to develop Gut feeling which is nothing but his conscience manifesting as voice of conscience. He is realized being, enjoying dance of nature.

*Comments attached*

# BOOK 1. UNDERSTAND, GOD & TRUTH

## 1. UNDERSTAND

**Shekhar Ray**

"All hypocrisy and diplomacy are trivial and mundane in life's journey." - that's why great masters suggest complete surrender as the best way. ........... although the same may be the 'escape route' for hypocrites.

**Somnath Banerjee in reply to Shekhar Ray**

Please understand that all hypocrisy and diplomacy gets day lighted with passage of time. Man is endowed with consciousness and conscience, your consciousness has to surrender to conscience.

**Gs Chawla**

NICE, You have to understand yourself & trust yourself -1.

**Somnath Banerjee in reply to Gs Chawla**

You are then a wise man.once understanding comes wisdom follows

**Gs Chawla in reply to Somnath Banerjee**

VERY TRUE SIR, Thanks

**Somnath Banerjee in reply to Gs Chawla**

So you are wise man. do not try to understand something undefinable.

**Sunil Jena**

Nice one

**Somnath Banerjee in reply to Sunil Jena**

Welcome

**Sudeep Chater**

Very nice blog.
Thanks for posting such useful information.
keep on posting more.

**Somnath Banerjee in reply to Sudeep Chater**

Yes understanding shall continue.
thanks for encouragement

*Abc Narayan*
Learn from everything and understand the TRUTH is the SPIRITUALITY; and, putting it into practice is the NOBILITY, and the result will be the DIVINE GRACE.

*Somnath Banerjee in reply to Abc Narayan*
EXCELLENT obsn, Understanding is a relation between the knower and an object of understanding.

Everybody make you understand but nobody understand you.

*Abc Narayan in reply to Somnath Banerjee*
Very true observation.

Thanks, and regards.

*Somnath Banerjee in reply to Abc Narayan*
Hope you understand, regards

*Abc Narayan in reply to Somnath Banerjee*
My simplicity and minus side (below zero side) ego does not allow me to say - ' I UNDERSTAND' because the applicability of the word 'UNDERSTAND' is comparative, and that need not be a finite. So, I pressume that it is upto others to consider and evaluate what I UNDERSTOOD.
Thanks, and regards.

*Somnath Banerjee in reply to Abc Narayan*
Ego cannot be negative as it is image created by you, all good and bad attributed are additive. even you are able to erase some of them yet it cannot go negative.understanding is not comparative, when you partially understand it means you understand part of the process and you dont understand rest of it.

*Abc Narayan in reply to Somnath Banerjee*
I neither want to involve in any arguement, nor interested to add to my already expressed view in this subject. What I iike to say here only is that as in this world there are so many countries nearly around 200 of them, and different country is having their own different views on most matters world affairs and national and local policies. And as per my view one of the main factor which contrubutes for the type of view in a person is that persons economic status and up bringing. Similary though India altogether is a single country but

in fact in social nature like liberal, conservative, and many other attitude one can say that India is a group of many countries with people of very diversified views. So, invoving in any agruements is a futile attempt in consideration of various ego levels in different people of different social culture whether the ego is of negative type or of positive type, or as you said - only one type, and it in one direction only.

Let us rest the matter here itself.
Thanks, and regards,
/abcn.

### Somnath Banerjee in reply to Abc Narayan
Seeker of ST you can always have your view. you can agree to disagree. yet aim is to understand and remove ambiguity. may lord help you.

## 3 KNOW YOUR BEING

**Dolphin** The rise or fall, the fame or infame, the make or break, life or struggle. ......all are attributed to one's self more than any other influences, long as you are capable of being self & believing in self you wont get regretted. ......

### Somnath Banerjee in reply to Dolphin
Dualities end when you know your being

### Somnath Banerjee in reply to Abhijit Nath
Nothing good or bad about it
know yourself

### Pushpa Chaturvedi
Nice messages
Knowing self is the first step to happiness

### Somnath Banerjee in reply to Pushpa Chaturvedi
Knowing self is happiness.
Gita ch2,65
A disciplined person, enjoying sense objects
With senses that are under control
And free from likes and dislikes,
Attains tranquillity.
All sorrows are destroyed
Upon attainment of tranquillity.

***Pushpa Chaturvedi in reply to Somnath Banerjee***
True
Keeping senses under control means killing desired which are the main cause of our sorrow
Please share
http://www.speakingtree.in/public/spiritual-blogs/ seekers/ pilgrimage/a-republic-day-message

***Somnath Banerjee in reply to Pushpa Chaturvedi***
Enjoy sense object with discipline -know yourself

***Pushpa Chaturvedi in reply to Somnath Banerjee***
True. Thank you

***Somnath Banerjee in reply to Pushpa Chaturvedi***
Welcome

## 5. DEFINATION OF GOD (QUANTUM PHYSICS)

***Bikash Mukherjee***
We love to believe and stay under a powerful one,the creator, God. May be acceptance is peace.

***Somnath Banerjee in reply to Bikash Mukherjee***
Get rid of slave mentality, nature has endowed with sufficient power to survive,grow and reproduce. Peace - static in dynamic domain- is figment of imagination, peace you get only at the end.

***Bikash Mukherjee in reply to Somnath Banerjee***
Very true, Who is who, Nature or God? People love to listen such words. What harm if people are happy to use their imaginary power? Let there be peace of mind.

***Somnath Banerjee in reply to Bikash Mukherjee***
Mind is never at peace even while sleeping brain activity can be measured. thoughts are generated from external stimuli and internal brain complexes. A dedicated effort is required to maintain peace in mind. Nature is manifestation of God, an expected value in the ambience of earth.

***Bikash Mukherjee in reply to Somnath Banerjee***
Slavery in our mind. We are slave of time and nature.

*Somnath Banerjee in reply to Bikash Mukherjee*
True, human are the only species with unlimited intelligence and
your mind has capacity to transcend both nature and time. when
time ceases spectrum of life can be visualised and slavery of mind
disappears

*Anu Kriti*
Gr8 interpretation

*Somnath Banerjee in reply to Anu Kriti*
Are your ambiguity clear?

*Pavan Raina*
I bow to your thought and the poem which you have crafted. Just
reading and understanding the essence gave me inner peace, such a
pleasant feeling. I am not joking sir.Thanks.

*Somnath Banerjee in reply to Pavan Raina*
Thanks,my experiences have made me humble.

## 8 WHEN MAN CREATED GOD

*Susil Kumar Bandopadhyay*
Thanks for the article "Man created God".

*Somnath Banerjee in reply to Susil Kumar Bandop...*
Welcome, i hope it meets some of your queries

*N A Ramachandra Pai*
Actually could you enlighten further in this matter. When how did
all this happen or are you writing just for sake of writing.

*Somnath Banerjee in reply to N A Ramachandra Pa...*
Any point not in conformity with the scripture

*Somnath Banerjee in reply to N A Ramachandra Pa...*
Did my analysis not meeting yours? you are at liberty to educate
me.

*Somnath Banerjee in reply to N A Ramachandra Pa...*
I am seeker of truth and donot write for writing. game of life
depicted in the slide is computer aided game.Stefan Hawkin in his
book the grand design. has explained the concept. if you have any
more inquiry i would try to answer them

Vivekananda in his book jnan jog has clearly highlighted development of religion and concept of God, blog gives the latest view of GOD

### Shri Dattaswami

The existence of God need not be known from the scriptures. If the scripture alone is the authority for the existence of God, nobody will believe it since any imaginary story can be created by any book. The practical observations of nature revealed the existence of God and scripture is only a record of the conclusions of debates of scientists, who observed the nature and events of life. When the nature was observed, the biggest surprise was about the infiniteness of space without the boundary wall of the universe. This is a practical enquiry raising anxiety in the minds of the observers of the nature, who are called as scientists.

After several debates, the conclusion was that the boundary of the universe is unimaginable since the space is infinite. An international conference on the diameter of the universe was held in which several theories were proposed and the essence of all the theories was only that the universe is infinite on all sides. Some proposed constant expansion of the universe, which also does not give the correct idea of the unimaginable boundary of the space. One scientist asked that even if the boundary wall of the universe is found by travelling 200 billion light years, which is the supposed diameter of the universe, what should be present after the boundary wall? About 200 research papers were presented and the final conclusion was only that the universe is infinite and its boundary wall is unimaginable. This unimaginable boundary of the universe is called as God. The unimaginable boundary of the universe must not contain any space and should not have spatial dimensions. Then only it becomes unimaginable.

Any entity having even very very small spatial dimensions can be imaginable. If the boundary is imaginable, you are still continuing in the imaginable phase of universe only and the boundary should not be reached. If the boundary has no spatial dimensions, it should be the generator of the space. The reason is that space cannot exist in its generator before its generation. This point again mutually proves that the boundary is the generator of space. Therefore, the existence of unimaginable boundary called as unimaginable God is not mere imagination of some scriptures. It is the conclusion of most practical observations of the infinite space or universe. Added to this concept, sometimes some unimaginable events called as miracles are observed in the life, which cannot be rejected as magic. Whether the miracles, which are unimaginable events, are believed or not, the unimaginable boundary of the universe cannot be rejected at any cost. Therefore, the boundary of the universe is not only unimaginable, but also happens to be the generator of space or universe.

Therefore, the concept of God is the result of deep scientific analysis of practical observation of nature only.

The devotees may be wrong. But you should think that how much wrong will be the devotee in absence of faith in God, which results in fear for sin that is punishable in terrible hell. You must have the relative imagination and be satisfied with the relatively controlled cheating of the devotees due to faith in God. God never does any miracle to remove the bad behaviour of human beings. The realisation should come in the minds of the people, which alone results in permanent transformation and for this purpose God comes down again and again in human form to preach the divine spiritual knowledge for the sake of such transformation. Such transformation alone is real for which God is always trying through human incarnations. You must appreciate that the concept of God develops fear for sin and brings the inbuilt resistance to crime in every heart of the individual. The concept of God also brings confidence and patience in your heart avoiding the depression of mind due to the victory of injustice. Otherwise, the patience is not developed, which leads to the birth of terrible concepts like terrorism that bring chaos in the society. You must appreciate the concept of God from the scientific analysis of nature and its tremendous benefits in the administration of the balance of individuals and social balance at large. If you throw away the concept of God treating it as theoretical imagination, the society would have been blasted by now in to pieces.

### *Somnath Banerjee in reply to Shri Dattaswami*
The existence of God need not be known from the scriptures.'
there are scriptures which is not cognitive of GOD like Buddhism etc

This unimaginable boundary of the universe is called as God. ' Gita says the whole universe is nothing but God and not only its unimaginable boundry. If you can imagine 200billion light year why not its boundary.

You must appreciate that the concept of God develops fear for sin and brings the inbuilt resistance to crime in every heart of the individual. Both are being concocted by man for maintenance of society.

Every man is potentially divine. that unimaginable boundary of universe cannot incarnate in human form long time I am seeing your comment, How are you

### *Shri Dattaswami in reply to Somnath Banerjee*
The world is in Me, I am not in the world, the world is also not in Me.....

There are three statements in the Gita. i) The world is in Me, ii) I am not in the world and iii) The world is also not in Me (Matsthani sarva bhutani, na chaham teshvavasthitah, na cha matsthani bhutaani, nattvaham teshu te mayi...). God happens to be the unimaginable boundary of the imaginary world on all sides. The area of the room is within the four walls. It is not beyond the four walls. It means it is in the control of the boundary wall.

Though the area is within the boundary wall, it is not present inside the wall. The boundary wall is also not in the area of the room since the boundary wall is outside the room. We say that an island is in the sea. It means that the island is surrounded by the sea on all sides like the boundary wall. It does not mean that the sea is in the island.

At the same time, when a sunk boat is immersed in the sea, we also say that the sunk boat is in the sea. The sea water is present in the sunk boat. In both cases, we have used the same type of sentence that the island or sunk boat is in the sea. There is similarity in the statement but there is difference in the situation since the sea water exists in the sunk boat and not in the island. Here, the universe is said to be in God like the island in the sea. The God is not in the world, which means that the sea water is not in the island. Hence, the case here is not the sunk boat. But, by the similarity of the construction of the sentence in both cases that both are in the sea, you may misunderstand that the island is in the sea like the sunk boat. In such case, it is negated by saying that the world is not in the God like the sunk boat in the sea.

Neither the unimaginable God exists in the imaginable world to make the world also unimaginable nor the imaginable world exists in unimaginable God to make God as imaginable. If God is in the world everywhere, the difference between good and bad becomes impossible. However, this does not mean that God cannot enter the world. As a general rule, God is not in the world. But, the omnipotent God can enter the world by entering a selected human being to make the human incarnation. The process of the entry is also unimaginable since the actions of God are also unimaginable. The human incarnation remains imaginable in the external medium but becomes unimaginable in certain specific actions. Since God is not in any item of the world, every item of the world is rejected as God as said in the Veda (Neti Neti...).

Every imaginable item in the world exhibits only imaginable characteristics due to absence of unimaginable God in it. At the same time, God enters the world through a selected specific human being to become human incarnation as said in the Veda (Tadevanu pravishat...) and this shows the omnipotency of God rejecting that He cannot enter the world. It is true that He did not enter the world. It is not true if you say that He cannot enter the world. The Veda says that He can enter any item in the world (Eeshaavaasyamidam...) and this statement is misunderstood as the statement meaning that He entered every item in the world. In this way, the contradiction in the statements of the Gita can be resolved.

### Somnath Banerjee in reply to Shri Dattaswami
God enters the world through a selected specific human being to become human incarnation'

Every human being is potentially divine. each one is endowed with voice of conscience. only your ego does notpermit you to listen to it. you can develop like a magician certain traits which people may attribute to god. only person you are fooling is yourself.

there is no ambiguity in gita, they appear so when quoted out of context. quantum mechanically the eigen function is omnipresent but its potential changes with the Hamiltonian that it operates on, the expected value iis also operated by the eigen function. lost in delusion we fail to see the truth. you may read quantum entanglement, spacial disposition and time integration to clear ambiguity existing in your mind

### Shekhar Ray
Man created God not only to blame him for everything but also to give all credit for everything !

### Somnath Banerjee in reply to Shekhar Ray
Blame and credit go hand in hand. when you blame someone for everything you automatically credit him for everything. good observation, thanks

## 11. BRAHM SATYA JAGAT MITHYA ?

### Sunita Gupta
That is truth which has not changed and what is that truth ----- we all need to find our own truths but then satya is. ............nice exploration and nicely written blog !!

### Somnath Banerjee in reply to Sunita Gupta
The invariance of the dynamic system may be defined as the truth of the system

## 13. ALL LOGIC.EMOTION AND ACTION ARE TRUE

### Ranganathan Ganapathy
Man's immortality in service, must be experienced and felt in nature and soul, and not merely understood by his intellectual faculties. True evidences come through two inward sources of wisdom— intuition and reflection.

Those who dare to be truthful to these inward sources of knowledge will feel positive evidence of immortality, and external evidences will serve but as illustrations. When you find this internal conviction of immortality which no sophistry can invalidate, you have found a treasure beyond all price.

Between the reality of birth and death, is life, and all actions need to be humanity oriented.

***Somnath Banerjee in reply to Ranganathan Ganapa...***
Researchers at Harvard University found that people with a more intuitive thinking style tend to have stronger beliefs in God than those with a more reflective style. Intuitive thinking means going with one's first instinct and reaching decisions quickly based on automatic cognitive processes. Reflective thinking involves the questioning of first instinct and consideration of other possibilities, thus allowing for counterintuitive decisions. both are decision making process, fundamental algorithm of nature, they also wax and wane. they are true and can be evaluated. these are in mental domain may not be valid in spiritual domain. life per se must be understood as truth, then imortality of life shall be evident..

thanks for your addition.

## 14. BEING CUSTODIAN DON'T ACT LIKE OWNER

***Bikash Mukherjee***
Nice.Came empty handed and will go empty handed.

***Somnath Banerjee in reply to Bikash Mukherjee***
True, but life lies between these bound state

Dr
Very good poem.

Infact man is not owner of anything, wealth, woman or any pleasantries. He is not an owner of himself even. There is nothing like ' I '. Man is just a custodian, and that too, is nothing but a combination of time, space and matter. Man has no right to sacrifice any thing, at the same time he has no power to cause any harm to anybody.

So is life. But you have concluded well in very positive way, in these words : You are otherwise numb but your eyes shine.

Good lines, good message.
Congratulations.
Regards.

**Somnath Banerjee in reply to Dr**
True but Objectivism says there is nothing but I.

**Dr in reply to Somnath Banerjee**
Yes. That's equally true. It always happens when we look at anything with various ' isms ' and thoughts.

Regards.

**Somnath Banerjee in reply to Dr**
What is then truth - the unchangeable

**Dr in reply to Somnath Banerjee**
So far truth is concerned it manifests in various ways in various beliefs and isms. It is also believed that no one has known the truth uptil now.

Strange but it is also said that the truth is that whose opposite is also truth.

Emperor Ashok, emperor Akbar and many others like them tried their best to know the truth. But were never satisfied with any answer.

**Somnath Banerjee in reply to Dr**
The truth is that whose opposite is also truth. ' Not understood

**Dr in reply to Somnath Banerjee**
I am afraid, but for this I would suggest you to google truth and then opposite of it.

I will give here few examples :

1. One should not kill anybody ; one should kill one's enemy ( in war ).

2. Death is end of life, there is life after death.

3. Life is full of suffering ; life is full of joy.

And so on.

**Dr**
I have just written a comment on a blog which you might find a little bit relevant. it is as follows :

"Yes, a nice blog. Well presented in slides. But I am afraid to say that experience varies from person to person. No. 2. Seeing something is an experience but a very limited experience. Because, when we see something, we actually see what we look for. We ever see the whole that's available to us. Hence our experience is also a part experience. Practically we often miss the main part of something which we see. But still, I agree that seeing is experiencing. And that has its effects."

It is on Mr. Bipin Chandr Pathi's blog, ' life free from despair. ... Today only. just now.

**Somnath Banerjee in reply to Dr**
I agree that seeing is experiencing' seeing is part of direct perception it becomes experience when intellect operates on it and suggests to ego to accept or veto, if accepted the perception is broken into attributes and functions. these are stored in different brain complexes. this then serves as experience

**Dr in reply to Somnath Banerjee**
Yes. Agreed.

## 15 DON'T BELIEVE WHAT YOU SEE

**Ron Krumpos**
In spirituality, "gut feeling" is better described as "intuitive insight." Intuition plays an important role in the mysticism of all religions; it gives an insight into the divine essence. Intuitive insight, looking without or within, is just a prelude to divine union. Looking without, expanded consciousness of matter allows us to realize its spiritual quintessence and ours. Looking within, greater consciousness of our own divine essence enables us to realize it in all matter. These are two approaches to one goal: experiencing divine Reality.

**Sangameswaran Nurani in reply to Ron Krumpos**
Can you kindly, for my benefit, elaborate a little more on "looking within and looking without" concepts Sir.? Thank you. Thanks and Regards.

**Somnath Banerjee in reply to Sangameswaran Nura...**
'looking within and looking without' concept propounded by Lord Budha, It has also been amplified by Krishnamurthy. your senses are designed look out but how do you perceive an object? your eyes cant see when you are dead. your perception depends on mind. looking without : senses bring in input and mind interprets it. itcan be improved by training like clarity and resolution. e.g. you look at a woman but through a bush. looking within : here the perception of mind is independent of the senses, here mind may examine memory domains, intellect, ego etc. it has no limit. this is very elementary. hope it meets your requirement

**Sangameswaran Nurani in reply to Somnath Banerjee**
Yes. Thanks.

**Somnath Banerjee in reply to Sangameswaran Nura...**
Welcome

**Somnath Banerjee in reply to Ron Krumpos**
Nothing comes from nothing and nothing comes by chance.

Gut feeling is more simple than intuitive insight.

Gut feeling is spontaneous while intuitive insight has to developed,

intuitive insight is part of your intellect while Gut feeling is Voice of conscience.

At some level they may merge with each other.

**Sangameswaran Nurani in reply to Somnath Banerjee**
"Nothing comes from nothing and nothing comes by chance" is the very basis of the Universe. Everything has a purpose, though we may not know them, because we are also part of the system and we think within that system.

**Somnath Banerjee in reply to Sangameswaran Nura...**
True. but when you are being rocked by the wave you cant see it, to appreciate the waves you are to be out of it. so transcend the mode of nature and enjoy the beauty of nature.

### Sangameswaran Nurani
Sir. Very nice presentation. Think you were in infantry, by the way. I do not know whether my Gut Feeling is correct. An Infantry Officer turns spiritual by his actions in the field very fast as compared to a person theoretically attempting to learn spirituality!!!! If I have taken little liberty with you, please excuse me Sir. I am saying this, as I said, from my Gut feeling.

### Somnath Banerjee in reply to Sangameswaran Nura...
Indian Military Academy trains officers of all arns and services. Since he does not live in society he is either animal or God, when he retires Animalism is over he becomes GOD.

Best of luck for Gut feeling

### Sangameswaran Nurani in reply to Somnath Banerjee
Sir, very nicely put with lot of philosophical contents. Fortunately, I have come across men in services, though very briefly, and very young that too, and find most of them are representatives of GOD. I am not over exaggerating; as their qualities of head and heart are at a higher level. May God bless them with more courage and enthusiasm, in whose hands safety of our Mother Land can be trusted. Good luck to you Sir.

### Somnath Banerjee in reply to Sangameswaran Nura...
They are trained to be demi gods. sometime the power gained corrupt them.

### Rakesh Verma
Gut feeling is the voice of conscience. Very true.

But we tend to add wisdom to it before making the so called "prudent" decision.

The purity of the feeling thus gets coloured, biased, and loses track.

### Somnath Banerjee in reply to Rakesh Verma
As per Patanjali, you believe only by direct perception or inferred perception, When perception fail you refer to others. But for excelling in the field of action, the gut feeling is important. these are subconsciously programmed with multiple information, courses

of action and execution methodology. The Gut feeling comes with experience.

### Sunita Gupta
Very well concluded message of the blog --listen to to your gut feeling and that is the voice of soul.

### Somnath Banerjee in reply to Sunita Gupta
No apology for mind and body functioning.Thanks

### Sunita Gupta in reply to Somnath Banerjee
When you are truly vigilant to your soul. ..mind and body never invade you. they do so only when when you ignore the soul... anterman ki awaaz.

### Somnath Banerjee in reply to Sunita Gupta
'anterman ki awaaz. ' agree with you absolutely. it is soft and suggestive and accepts your veto. like loving mate very persuasive

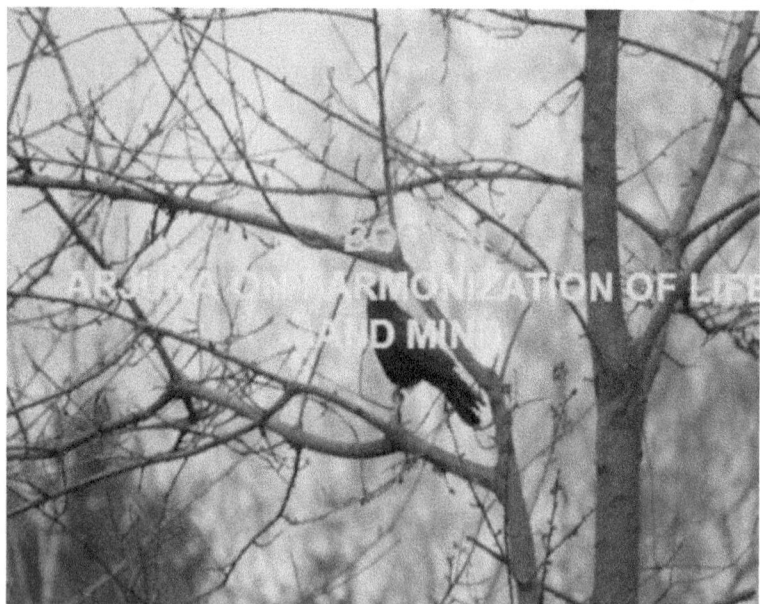
ARJUNA ON HARMONIZATION OF LIFE
AND MIND

# BOOK II
## ARJUNA ON HARMONIZATION OF LIFE AND MIND

## COMMENTS

# 16. WHAT IS THE USE OF THE KINGDOM, OR ENJOYMENT, OR EVEN LIFE? GITA (1.32)

The cost benefit analysis of human life reveal a tradeoff. The benefits both tangible and intangible demand sacrifice in terms of time, money and energy. The choices are yours. There are great people who have conquered the world at the cost of enjoyment and life (*Alexander the Great*). There are some who have sacrificed kingdom and life for enjoyment (*King* Edward VIII ) and there are humans who have sacrificed kingdom and enjoyment for sublimating life *(Buddha)*. The multitude still pay homage to them.

Lord Krishna's answer is well documented in Gita. Jesus and Buddha has answered in their own way.

Dear Seeker and Masters Of ST, can you answer the question from our living standard or present way of life such that we be more efficient and our life be success.

*Comments attached*

# 17. HOW CAN WE BE HAPPY AFTER KILLING OUR KINSMEN?

Arjuna's question What pleasure shall we find in killing the sons of Dhritaraashtra? How can we be happy after killing our kinsmen?

Krishna responds

Shake off this weakness of your heart
And get up (for the battle), O Arjuna.

And a host of reasons for fighting but no reason for loss of pleasure and happiness.

Killing action which strikes us as terrible or pitiable must happen between persons who are either friends or enemies or indifferent to one another. If an enemy kills an enemy, there is nothing to excite pity either in the act or in the intention. Same is the case with indifferent person, but when the tragic incident occurs between those who are near or dear to one another, i.e a brother kills, or indents to kill a brother, a son his father etc are situation that invoke pity.

Exampleis from bible "As a test for Abraham, God demands the sacrifice of his son, Isaac. That sacrifice is forestalled just as Abraham raises the knife."

My dear Seekers and Masters can you answer the question posed by Arjun.

'Can you be happy after killing your Kins"

*Comments attached*

# 18. WHY SHOULDN'T WE, WHO CLEARLY SEE EVIL IN THE DESTRUCTION OF THE FAMILY, THINK ABOUT TURNING AWAY FROM THIS SIN?

Disgusted by the senseless killing and wastage of war, Arjuna at the beginning of a great battle throws down his weapons and refuses to kill his brothers. Krishna persuades Arjuna that as a warrior his role is to fight, no matter how revolting the cause or pointless the deaths, the material world is not real, and life and death are twin illusions.

Today We have lost our "moral compass" with society blighted by selfishness, greed and family breakdown, These and other modern-day "social evils" have destroyed traditional, shared values and left people feeling a deep sense of unease,It criticises the Government, big business, religion and the media for the unwelcome changes which now shape our society., Drugs and alcohol, crime and violence, poverty and inequality as the things we are worried. we are concerned about the way our society has become more individualistic, greedy and selfish, seemingly at a cost to our sense of community, Connected to all of these issues was the perception that we no longer share a set of common values and that we have lost our 'moral compass Everything seems to be based around money and owning things. The more you have, the more successful you are. there's nothing wrong with having enough, but there's pressure on people to go for more and more. youth culture for anti-social behaviour, binge-drinking, violence, gun and knife crime, they were failed by their families, schools and the media.

My question to you is

1. Have we lost moral Compass? Is religion responsible for it.

2. Is destruction of family, a forgivable sin?

*Comments attached*

## 19. I REQUEST YOU TO TELL ME, DECISIVELY, WHAT IS BETTER FOR ME. I AM YOUR DISCIPLE. TEACH ME WHO HAS TAKEN REFUGE IN YOU. (2.07)

A natural desire to surrender to a greater experience than one's own occurs. An experience of true surrender is a source of immense joy and leads one through the last barriers set up by the ego. This is where one needs the doorway to step out of the illusion and the doorway is the Teacher. The two finally become One.

Krishna introduces Dharma and Atma

Dharma may be defined as the eternal law governing, upholding, and supporting the creation and the world order. It also means duty, righteousness, ideal conduct, moral principles, and truth. Adharma is an antonym to Dharma.

Expert guidance should be sought during the moment of crisis

Atma or Atman means consciousness, spirit, soul, self, the source of life and the cosmic power behind the body-mind complex. Just as our body exists in space, similarly our thoughts, intellect, emotions, and psyche exist in Atma, the space of consciousness. Atma cannot be perceived by the senses, because, the senses abide in Atma.

Philosophers enter into a controversy. Some enquire how such a philosophical discourse could take place at the commencement of a war. How was it possible? There are others who firmly hold that this momentous discourse was not only possible but inevitable at that hour,

Even today a commander briefs his subordinate commanders and his men before commencement of any hostility on mission, enemy, courses of action and execution orders.

Express your views without inhibition.

*Comments attached*

## 20. WHAT IS THE MARK OF A PERSON WHOSE PRAJNA IS STEADY AND MERGED IN SUPERCONSCIOUS STATE? HOW DOES A PERSON OF STEADY PRAJNA SPEAK? HOW DOES SUCH A PERSON SIT AND WALK? GITA 2.54

Shifting the awareness from the experience to the experiencer; since all the experiences are on the circumference and they keep on changing. The experiencer is at the centre. Again and again come back to the experiencer.

Characteristics of wise men

1. *Does this person show evidence of grace through a generosity of spirit, a love for mercy, an ability to forgive?*

2. *Does this person have a good reputation with others; is he or she the kind of person others seek out for advice and support?*

3. *Does this person live a consistent life? Where there is wisdom, there is stability.*

4. *Does this person show a reasonable breadth of thought?*

5. *Does this person show a depth of thought?*

6. *Would other people describe this person as fair-minded?*

7. *Has this person learned some lessons in life through hard times?*

"Everyone then who hears these words of mine and does them will be like a wise man who built his house on the rock. And the rain fell, and the floods came, and the winds blew and beat on that house, but it did not fall, because it had been founded on the rock. Matthew 7:24-25

Gita recommend knowledge, action, devotion equamity and surrender to be wise man.

So, what according to you is wisdom.?

*Comments attached*

## 21. IF YOU CONSIDER THAT TRANSCENDENTAL KNOWLEDGE IS BETTER THAN WORK THEN WHY DO YOU WANT ME TO ENGAGE IN THIS HORRIBLE WAR, GITA 3.1-2

Question of essence

The question is essence of Gita. Question of essence is that probe for deeper meaning and set the stage for further questioning foster the development of critical thinking skills and higher order capabilities such as; problem solving, and the understanding of complex systems

Krishna"s answer

Krishna;s Answer always perform your duty efficiently and without attachment to the results,because by doing work without attachment one attains the Supreme.

Today's socially Democaric way of living i.e. "For the People, By the People, Of the People" need to under go change, as it gives rise to feeling of "karta"(I am doing) whereas Geeta says you are not Doing anything and "Karak is the Supreme Lord "

Ponder and answer
1. When is transcendental knowledge better than work?

2. To engage in this horrible war', Are not all war horrible?

3. Do modes of nature allow work without attachment?

4. Do transcendental knowledge have any reparations in the physical domain of human life.

5. Was Gandhari right in accusing Krishna for getting her 100 son killed. Please be free to express your views, so that we may understand Karma Yog better.

*Comments attached*

## 22. YOU SEEM TO CONFUSE MY MIND BY APPARENTLY CONFLICTING WORDS. TELL ME, DECISIVELY, ONE THING BY WHICH I MAY ATTAIN THE SUPREME. (GITA 3.2)

Krishna replied

One who sees the path of renunciation
And the path of work as the same, really sees.

Both lead to the Supreme

Isa Upanishad goes on to say, «He who knows both knowledge and action, with action overcomes death, and with knowledge reaches immortality.» (Knowledge and action are two types of Yoga (Union with the Divine), Jnana (Knowledge) and karma (Action). The other types are Hatha (physical), Bhakti (Love), and Rajah (Mystical Experience).)

According to Soumen De in his essay on "The Historical Context of the Bhagavad-Gita and Its Relation to Indian Religious Doctrines," Karma is "The law of universal causality, which connects man with the cosmos and condemns him to transmigrate -- to move from one body to another after death -- indefinitely. In the Gita, Krishna makes an allusion to the eternal soul that moves from body to body as it ascends or descends the ladder of a given hierarchy, conditioned on the nature of one's own karma -- work of life or life deeds."

Gita is to ensure efficiency in our life's battle.

Knowledge without action leads to accelerated degradation of life function.

Action without knowledge shall lead to chaos.

Knowledge with action lead to devotion entails surrender and salvation.

## 23. REINCARNATION

"How am I to understand That You taught this yoga (karma yoga) in the beginning?

Krishna said:

Both you and I have taken many births. I remember them all, O Arjuna, But you do not remember.

A Vedantin believes in Brahman, the Law of karma, reincarnation, maya, and the Atman or divine spark within man. Reincarnation is one of the central concept[ of Gita.

Carl sagan asked theDalai Lama what he would do if a fundamental tenet of his religion (reincarnation) were definitively disproved by science. The Dalai Lama answered, «If science can disprove reincarnation, Tibetan Buddhism would abandon reincarnation... but it's going to be mighty hard to disprove reincarnation".

Belief in reincarnation is held by adherents of almost all major religions except Christianity and Islam. Hindus provide reasons for reincarnation. they are to experience the fruits of one's karmas: to satisfy one's desires: to complete one's unfinished sadhana, to fulfil a debt: to undergo sufferings because of a great soul's curse and to attain moksha: Buddhist texts make it clear that there is no permanent consciousness that moves from life to life

Though the major Christian denominations reject the concept of reincarnation, a large number of Christians profess the belief. In a survey in 2009, 24% of American Christians expressed a belief in reincarnation

Reincarnation is widely accepted by the major Eastern religions -- most prominently Hinduism and Buddhism. It also has a history in ancient Greek philosophy. However, for people more familiar with the major monotheistic religions -- Christianity, Judaism and Islam -- the idea of reincarnation seems foreign and maybe even a little strange. That's because Christianity, Judaism and Islam conceive of time linearly. Life is simply a short step that determines the quality of an afterlife. For those who believe in only one life followed by an eternal afterlife, reincarnation is like an unwieldy marathon run by relay instead of a short, concise sprint.

Dear Seekers and Masters of Speaking tree

1. What valuable lessons we can learn from the teaching of reincarnation.
2. How is Karma Yog related to Reincarnation?
3. what are the impediments in disproving reincarnation.
4. how can you justify immortality of life?

*Comments attached*

## BOOK II
## ARJUNA ON HARMONIZATION OF LIFE AND MIND

### 16. ARJUNA What is the use of the kingdom,
### or enjoyment, or even life?

*Somnath Banerjee*
Arjuna had asked Lord Krishna more than two dozen questions in Bhagbath Gita,I request you to give new meaning to it

*Saroj Das*
Thanks. Which one first..! ☺☺ It is because...answering all his questions = the LORD'S complete song..., the Gita. Or.. .do you like to have the (not new) true meaning of Krishna's answers? Thanks. Love.sd//

*Somnath Banerjee*
i would very much appreciate the true meaning
thanks & regards

*Saroj Das*
Thanks for seeking the true meaning......
May the true meaning of Gita settle in everyone's Intellect !
Regards.

Here is my understanding of the Gita.
Regards.

"The blessed Lord says through the mouth of Sri Krishna that "beings, who seem to be manifest in the middle are actually unmanifest before and again unmanifest after".(2/28).

'To project from the unmanifest to the manifest' is the program of creation of a thing, strictly following the Law of Causation.

When scholars ponder over this theory, the general observation is that "one sees This as a wonder; another speaks of This as a wonder; another hears of This as a wonder; yet, having heard none understands This at all!" (2/29).

True knowledge makes a man andrak that he is 'The Soul with a body', but now in his ignorance, he thinks that he is a 'body with a soul'. If you want to know THIS in the true sense of the term (tatwatah), Sri Bhagawan says,

"Know That by long prostration, by question, and service, the 'wise' who has seen the *Truth will instruct you in (that) knowledge". (4/34).*

*Remenber, one in a million becomes a Tatwadarshi. According to Sri Bhagwan's estimation "Among thousands of men, one per chance, strives for perfection; even among those successful strivers, only one per chance knows Me in essence" (7/3). (1000 x 1000) ! What is That essential knowledge?*

*Sri Bhagwan declares, "I shall declare to thee in full this knowledge combined with andrake, which being known, nothing more here remains to be known". (7/2).*

*This is the knowledge of YOGA, and not the knowledge of any secular science. Therefore appropriately Sri Bhagwan declares that "The Yogi is thought to be superior to the ascetics, and even superior to scholars (Gyaani); he is also superior to men-of-action; therefore (you strive to) be a Yogi, O Arjuna". (6/46).*

*If one is in the path of Yoga, Sri Bhagwan assures, "Knowing these paths, O Partha, no Yogin is deluded; therefore, AT ALL TIMES be yoked to Yoga (be steadfast in yoga) O, Arjuna". (8/27).*

*Otherwise, let it be known that "There is no Knowledge (of the Self) to the one who is not yoked (unyoked!); and to the unyoked no meditation; and to the unmeditative no peace; to the peaceless, how can there be happiness"?? (2/66).*

*love, dada ! Prasna ti daaroon chhilo!* ☺☺

*sd//*

### Somnath Banerjee

*You have brought out the solution provided by Lord Krishna beautifully. Thanks but you have not replied to the questionDear can you answer the question from our living standard or present way of life such that we be more efficient and our life be success.*

**Saroj Das**

*thanks a lot.*

*2. To those two dozen questions....., may i chose some important ones and answer / explain part by part ? Else, it becomes a volume.* ☺

*One such question is," atah kena prayukat ayam paapam charati purusha"..... or influenced by which factor man commits sin.., by force, as if" ?*

*And the Lord answers, It is the Kaama and the Krodha:... etc.*

*Sir, these things require elaborate explanation.* :☺

*Thanks,*
*sd//*

**Saroj Das**

*kindly refer to verse 36 and 37 of karmayoga, ch. 3.*

*The laws of the Gita is applicable to people belonging to any ear ! Sanatan laws!!*

*Arjuna in the Geeta, wants to know from the Lord about the exact factor / factors in the inner constituition of Man which, andrak the man to commit sin though, against his wish, but as if by force.The Lord not only introduces the Satan to Arjuna, but also describes in detail about the exact hide- outs from where this dangerous bandit sabotages the peace and knowledge of the individual.*

*The Lord says that it is the ' desire and anger' factor, which are born from ' a tendency to act' ( Rajo Guna), the most destructive and all – sinful. "Know this to be the enemy number one".*

*The sense organs, the mind and the intellect are its hide- outs and from these locations, it attacks and deludes the individual by veiling his wisdom. Therefore, one should first control the sense organs and kill this sinful thing; the destroyer of the individual's knowledge and wisdom.*

*One should properly undertstand that the sense organs are superior to the body ( of flesh and bones); the mind is superior to the sense organs; the intellect is even superior to the mind. In this sense, if the sense organs are the different outposts, mind is the commander and the den of the Satan; The Commander-in-Chief; (desire and anger); is the intellect.*

*Even superior to the intellect is He, the Atman.*

**Syed Hussain**

*Great one*

*Somnath Banerjee in reply to Syed Hussain*
*What does Koran say to the question"What is the use of the kingdom, or enjoyment, or even life?"*

**Tejinder Sidhu**
*MIND IS THE QUESTION AND SOUL/GOD IS THE ANSWER. MIND KEEPS ON GENRATING QUESTIONS AND EVERY ANSWER BECOMES ANOTHER QUESTION-THIS CHAIN OF QUESTIONS AND ANSWERS ENDS WITH ENLIGHTENMENT. WITH SOUL MERGING WITH GOD THERE IS NO EGO OR MIND TO ASK A QUESTION.*

**Somnath Banerjee in reply to Tejinder Sidhu**
*I agree, God is answer to all questions but it is a trivial solution as it does not improve efficiency or lead to success in life. when there is no ego you ceaze to exist*

## 17. HOW CAN WE BE HAPPY AFTER KILLING OUR KINSMEN?

**Saba Sharma**
*Mr. banerjee, interesting, thought provoking and actually mind blowing !*
*To the best of my knowledge and as you know, I don't know much ! ( I could not find the flowers either) !*

*The answer to both Questions is as follows : Krishna changed the mindset of Arjun to think beyond the Gross level ! Work is Worship ! Just Do your Dharma ! Fighting against unrighteousness is just ! and when these resonated with Arjuna, his mindset changed and the rest is history.*

*Now to add a modern twist, the same changing the mindset has been the cause of so many religious wars for better and worse, justified and unjustifiable !*

### Somnath Banerjee in reply to Saba Sharma
*I fully agree with you,*

*you shall be more efficient in performing your duty if you are not carried away by emotions.*

### Pavan Raina
*Arjun is metaphorically is the point of $3^{rd}$ chakra which is agni potent state and that why was agni putra. Below this state a person is more inclined towards materialism tendencies. This also means that till this stage the attachment with 5 senses and the mind and ego is too much. $3^{rd}$ chakra is a cross road and if one crosses this one goes in the higher plane and starts acquiring the knowledge of detachment. Hence this state is very important to cross to be closer to the truth. That is Arjun battling with his relatives signify the war with the senses which need to be overcome to seek the truth and be able to be with the almighty creator.*

*Yogananda has very nicely described it in his writing on GITA which I have tried to put in my words and that makes great sense to me.*

*Reply*

### Somnath Banerjee in reply to Pavan Raina
*Excellent summary of yogananda. the question is can you be happy after killing your kins.*

### Pavan Raina in reply to Somnath Banerjee
*Of course and that comes with evolution towards realization. I am not against with people obsessed with materialism and they are because they find enjoyment. Generation after generation people try to improving financially and try to seek the pleasure which western people have been given a picture of enjoying. Yes US sort of democratic nation where people are better secured for basic need by the govt people do have and had best of material pleasure but on the other hand people there are also fed up of this and see beyond.*

*They are the one who try to follow various hindu philosophy and follow from Rajneesh to Vivekananda. They are searching the pleasure of sat chit anand in their way. Not necessarily one has to have all the material fun and then think of satisfaction and then think for higher order pleasure. Once the kins are killed (sense) one may be closer to sat chit anand. I understanding if killing the kin is not permanently removing its entity but more important is winning the war which would mean I would use my senses as and when required and at that higher level f required for welfare of lifting some other souls. Such pleasure is not meant for all but one has to earn by karmas.*

### Somnath Banerjee in reply to Pavan Raina
*Please do correct kins are sense objects and senses are 10, five for perception and five for action. You are to control your senses not sense objects. So "one may be closer to sat chit anand'*

*your sense of bliss should not depend on ambient condition. so 'How can we be happy after killing our kinsmen? '*

### Pavan Raina in reply to Somnath Banerjee
*Dear Somnathjee you are correct and I am not so perfect is fine details but understand broadly which can make me help to practice a honest and peaceful life in this turbulent era. Well to answer your question Yoga nanda has very nicely defined not 5 nor 10 but 100 character of Mahabharat metaphorically of Kaurav which need to be controlled or killed. I also would like to have your perception or knowledge for my gain please.*

### Somnath Banerjee in reply to Pavan Raina
*Dear Pawan, i am like you a andra.*
*we help each bother in understanding the truth*

### Dr
*The conversation you refer was held in a battle-ground. Battle – ground of a war. Therefore first we must take up the word 'war '. What does it mean. How does it arise, how do two persons, two groups or two nation come to the stage of war with each other ? First of all let me know your idea or meaning of war, then may*

*be, we can find any answer. Please. .definition, a small definition will do.*

**Somnath Banerjee in reply to Dr**
*War is killing your enemies until any survivors surrender and do your will. War is a universal phenomenon whose form and scope is defined by the society that wages it.*
*you may refer to my blog Religion and War.*

**Dr in reply to Somnath Banerjee**
*I will certainly go through your valuable blog. Thanks for inviting me for that.*

*You have described some form of war. Perhaps I could not my question well. When I wanted to know your definition of war, I meant, what is the state of war. What you have written is, what happens in war. We have to go the very root of war, how does it emerges ?*

*What I feel," imposition of one's will over the other is war. "It is the idea of war, it is the origin of war, it is the basic cause of war, it is the initiation of war. Fighting is one aspect, there are cold wars also, sometimes much more dangerous than bloody fights. Fights are means of concluding a war.*

*Now, coming to your question, Kauravas and Pandavas came to a stage of war when kaurvas refused to give them a smallest piece of land. This was imposition of their strong will of negating all their rights upon the Pandavas. All doors of negotiations have already been knocked, in vain. So now what was left to the Pandavas except to fight, for their survival. They did not wish a war, but it was there before them and they had to face it, else perish completely. They were left with no option. When there is a war one has to face it, there is no other way out. Even Lord Ram waged a war over Rawan when all his efforts went in vain.. ..... That is why a war is not regarded as a good thing.*

**Somnath Banerjee in reply to Dr**
*The war envisaged is the war going in your mind.*

*All the entities in the brain can generate The vibrations in the mento-emotional energy (thought),*

*-one chain is external world – senses- mind- intellect- Ego – mind – organ of action. The other input is from soul- voice of conscience- Ego- mind-organ of action.. the knowledge and action is surrendered to devotion leads to surrendering Ego to soul that is realization.*

*the pleasure and happiness in the world are illusion and fleeting. Arjuna is living in physical domain. they have full dominance. The question therefore is "can you be happy after killing your Kins;*

### Dr in reply to Somnath Banerjee
*Let me try point wise.*

*1. It were kauravas who imposed their will of not granting the smallest piece of land to Pandavas, this was the andrake of the war. It was known to Pandavas only when kauravas declared war against them. A war that was inevitable.*

*2. Pandavas were left with no option but to face the war, by fighting it back.*

*3. Arjun raised several questions to Sri Krishna and showed his declination in facing the war.*

*4. In this course he raises the two questions, you have mentioned, in chapter 1 of Bhagwat Gita.*

*5. Sri Krishna replied to all his queries, including these two questions, telling him straight forwardly that there was in fact no killing at all.*

*6. Sri Krishna tells him both the possibilities of winning the war or losing it. And tells him that both the positions will be advantageous for him, because he will be fighting without any evil intention, he will just be doing his job as a warrior.*

*7. He tells Arjun that he won't have any pleasure or pain in doing it, because he will be doing it by nishkaam bhav. He tells him not to lament for any one also, with reasons.*

*8. Now, may I very humbly ask you what is the reason that you do not accept the whole answer given in the chapter 2. Of Bhagvat Gita. When in your last reply you have yourself accepted the Gita's version that pleasure and happiness are illusions.*

*9. The answer to both of your questions is, thus, there in Bhagvat Gita itself.*

*Thanking you.*

### Somnath Banerjee in reply to Dr

*Very true, Bhagwat Gita undoubtedly answer the question.. Pursuit of happiness is aim of life. You cannot brush it off by calling it illusions you may have different answer, bible gives different answer, so the question remains 'How can we be happy after killing our kinsmen?'*

### Dr in reply to Somnath Banerjee

*Happiness is not an illusion, I also believe that. I just mentioned that because you had referred that. Happiness matters, it is something else how one takes it, one can be happy by eating one Kg of sweets and someone else by distributing it.*

*1. In case of Arjun it wasn't a case of happiness, it was an uninvited situation in which he had to choose between ' to be killed ' or ' to kill ', not for any pleasure or happiness. Even today in some unfortunate situations some people fall in this type situation. What is expected of them, to save their life or let it go the enemy wishes.*

*2. Mahabhart is a mahakavy, a mythology, a story written by Vyaas Rishi. The purpose of writing such stories is to set an example before the people for their learning how to behave in an adverse situation, in a worst situation. As per the Karmyog point of view, Sri Krishna is depicted as telling what he found fit according to Karmyog. Of course there could be other possibilities also.*

*3. Ram did not fight with Bharat, that is another version where Maryadaa is supreme. Ram is high symbol of that and is regarded ' Maryaadaapurushottam ' and Sri Krishna is regarded as ' kar purushottam '. Both give a message of irradiating an evil, by two possible ways.*

*4. So far killing someone, not only one's kinsmen, any enemy, is not a matter of happiness, at least, Ramayan tells us only that. Ram went to Rishikesh to perform sever ' tap' for 'prayshchit ' for killing Ravan. How can we say Ram was happy by killing Ravan. Yes one can be happy by performing one's duty. Whatever it is. At least Sri Krishna also expected this from Arjun.*

*5. I tell you one more such a story. During the late times of Bahlol Lodi, his two sons were at war with each other. One of them, Sikander, who finally succeeded the war of succession, was once, before the war was over, visited by a Muslim saint. The saint very affectionately held one of Sikander's hand between his both the hands and said, "I wish your victory in the war with your brother ". Sikander was taken aback, he immediately withdrew his hand from the soft grip of the saint's hands and said," what are you saying, I get the victory, you should have said the one who would serve the people better should win ".*

*So we can say this does not provide any happiness to the victorious. But then every thing we do does not provide any happiness as well. All our actions are not for the happiness or pleasure,.*

*A police man, a judge, a soldier are not always happy after their every act. But then they do it. They do it because their duty demands it to be done.*

*You might have heard about Robespiere, a French dictator, during French Revolution, he was a sub court judge in his early life. In one case he was supposed to grant death penalty to the accused proved guilty, instead of doing so he resigned ant went home. But who knows the destiny. That man, after some time became one of the worst dictator of our times, for a period of almost one year, who got killed many innocent people during French Revolution. Finally he met the same fate. He, too, was killed to vacate his chair.*

*Does these people get any happiness by doing so, at least, I don't think so.*

### Somnath Banerjee in reply to Dr
*You have concluded that war does not lead to happiness.*
*then what are the spoils of war or humanity is wasting time for last 5000thousand years.*
*victory is intoxicant and habit forming.*

**Dr in reply to Somnath Banerjee**
*I wish you a very happy holi.*

*I haven't concluded anything as yet. May I request you to see my blog on war, ' a look at war ' on ST. http://www.speakingtree.in/ public/spiritual-blogs/ seekers/self-improvement/a-look-at-war*

**Somnath Banerjee in reply to Dr**
*Good blog, you have forgotton that there a war raging in your mind. Mind is Kurushetra. Vibrations from all domains have to be analysed, your ego and soul play a dominant part. Your success in life depends on it.*

**Dr in reply to Somnath Banerjee**
*Thanks. That's the advantage of this blog discussion, if one misses something some one is always there to supplement the missing parts. Yes, one's success depends on how one manages the war going in one's mind. Good addition. Thank you very much.*

**Somnath Banerjee in reply to Dr**
*Read my blog Religion and war in ST, you may add some more points to your own blog*

**Namo Fan**
*Very nice...*

**Somnath Banerjee in reply to Namo Fan**
*Thanks for your encouragement*

## 18. WHY SHOULDN'T WE, WHO CLEARLY SEE EVIL IN THE DESTRUCTION OF THE FAMILY, THINK ABOUT TURNING AWAY FROM THIS SIN?

**Shri Dattaswami**
*Arjuna came to Kurukshetra to fight with enemies in order to get back his kingdom. He thought that the war is his case and Krishna was helping him in his case like an advocate helping the petitioner in his case filed in a court. Arjuna thought that since he is the owner of the case, he can withdraw the case whenever he likes to do so. If the petitioner is not interested to fight the case, the advocate will have no interest to argue it. Arjuna thought that it was not proper to kill his grandfather and teacher for the sake of wealth. His*

*point was also justified. But, Krishna turned the tables diagonally opposite by enlightening Arjuna through the Gita. The analysis of Krishna revealed that the war was His work. Krishna revealed that He is God descended in human form on the earth (Manusheen Tanumashritam...) and wants to destroy the evil forces to establish justice.*

*Therefore, the war becomes the work of God. The advocate turned to be the petitioner of the case and therefore, the case cannot be withdrawn. If the petitioner turns away, the advocate will introduce his name in the name of the petitioner and the case will be re-filed in the court. Krishna made it clear that He is going to destroy the evil forces and since the grandfather and the teacher are the supporters of the injustice, both have to be also killed. Arjuna thought that it is better to kill the evil forces along with his grandfather and teacher and thereby, get the grace of God. If he withdraws from the war, both will not survive in any case and unnecessarily he will be the loser of the divine grace. Hence, he changed his opinion and fought the war.*

*Since God is greater than any worldly bond (Natatsamah... Veda), he was prepared to kill anybody for the sake of God. Except for this one valid point, Arjuna would have not fought even if the reason were the burning heart of his beloved wife, Draupadi. Now, the point is that the war is the work of God and not the materialistic work of Arjuna. The entire message of the Gita is in this context of the work done in the mission of God. Since the war is not the personal work of Arjuna, the message of the Gita cannot apply to the context of routine materialistic works. All the routine worldly works do not fall in the context of the Gita.*

*Only the works of God in which you participate come under the context of the Gita. Whenever you do the work of God, do not aspire any fruit from Him. The human being may forget the work done by you and may not reward you for your work but the omniscient and most generous God will never forget your work. If you aspire for the fruit, a limited fruit, which balances the value of your work will only be given by God. If you do not aspire, you will get unimaginable fruit. Draupadi bandaged the cut finger of Krishna with a piece of cloth torn from her sari and did not aspire for any fruit for doing that little service. Krishna gave her thousands of saris when she was attempted for unclothing.*

*Devotion of Arjuna and Hanuman*

*Arjuna, being a normal devotee with little faith in Krishna, participated in the work of God (Kurukshetra war) since it was a Holy Mission that helps the society in establishing the justice in the world. Hanuman was a super devotee with immense faith in Rama and hence, participated in the war, which was a personal work of God. The ultimate aim of your service should be to please the God, be it the social work or His personal work. Such devotion is perfect as in the case of Hanuman. The war in Kurukshetra was for the social welfare in one angle and was the personal work of Arjuna only and not at all the personal work of God. Therefore, the participation of Arjuna in the war does not involve high faith and high devotion.*

*In the case of Hanuman, it involves immense faith and devotion. You may think that the war was personal work of Rama in one angle and killing Ravana is social welfare in another angle and therefore, Hanuman participated in the war. Rama removed the second angle when He told that He will go back without killing Ravana if he returns Sita and now, the war was confined to the first angle only. In spite of the war exposed as the personal work of Rama only, Hanuman participated in the war and His aim was to please Rama without analyzing the nature of the work. Hence, Hanuman was rewarded with unimaginable fruit of becoming the future creator of the universe.*

*www.universal-spirituality.org*
*Universal Spirituality for World Peace*

**Somnath Banerjee in reply to Shri Dattaswami**
*1. 'that the war was His work. Krishna revealed ' very rightly brought out. Is there any war whether in field or in your mind, not work of lord- you are always an outside cause*

*2. Unnecessarily he will be the loser of the divine grace. ' Krishna said that Arjuna surrender to him then he would absolve him of his sins.*

*3.' All the routine worldly works do not fall in the context of the Gita.. '*

*Your mind is kurushetra where battle of life rages, gita provides modus –operandi to fight. Hence all actions are under purview of GITA.*

*4 your para 4 on unattached work though illuminating is not in the spirit of Gita, where cause and effect is applicable in physical domain only. Lord does not provide fruit of action only nature does..*

*5 devotion of arjuna and hanuman out of context of the present blog*

*I had expected that you would bring out the role of emotion in war.*

*regards*
**Rishi Ramesh Vishvas**

*Mr Somnath Banerjee ji..undoubtedly your blog is highlighting current scenario prevailing here not only in India,may be around the Globe.There may be more questions too arising into the mind.*

*There are innumerable solaces to satisfy as answers to raised questions,but solution is within our-self.*

*Irony is that once we have identified causes of unrest,we need to divert our full attention within us,since the least we are capable of doing is that we can certainly change/transform our-self only,once we start with our self,other's will follow us sooner or later.*

**Somnath Banerjee in reply to Rishi Ramesh Vishv...**
*What you say is true- a spiritual domain solution percolating to physical domain.*

*all religion advises the human to leave family*

*Jesus tells multitude only those to follow him who have left their family,*

*Buddha left family himself*

*so my question is- Have we lost moral Compass? Is religion responsible for it.*

*Is destruction of family, a forgivable sin?*

**Rishi Ramesh Vishvas in reply to Somnath Banerjee**
*Thanks for the response,though hinted very clearly and loudly,once again repeating it,there are hundreds of examples in spirituality who never denounced the world,remained with their respective families and yet got self enlightenment.Further real ''Guru'' is within us,in our heart,KNOW THYSELF–is the Religion....we may explore HIM at home living with the family.THERE IS ABSOLUTELY NO NEED TO GO ANY WHERE,as per your question,destruction/breaking of family or committing any sin or moral Compass.,which can be done at any place may be our own home,family,friends,relatives,huge circles,job,companies,shop,business,any domain etc...''Prabhu bhaav se parsann hote hain''.*

**Somnath Banerjee in reply to Rishi Ramesh Vishv...**
*'Know thyself' or introspection is an old concept of bygone era, it has never reached dominance or activated higher state of mind.*

*Attachment to Gold and Woman continues to be an impediment to self realization*

**Rishi Ramesh Vishvas in reply to Somnath Banerjee**
*What you are pointing out,it was even dominant in ''Satyug'',still rarest of rare chose the path of ''Self actualization'',like today,in 'Kalyug'..It's just one's choice.Since God has given us full liberty either to be a god or reverse of it..*

*thanks for the response.*

**Somnath Banerjee in reply to Rishi Ramesh Vishv...**
*''Self actualization'' falls under hierarchy of need,(Maslow) when your physical, social and safety needs are met.*

*Family is social need and must be met before self actualization need/*

**Rishi Ramesh Vishvas in reply to Somnath Banerjee**
*Strange,west always looking towards east, preferably India as a crusader for peace,relationship,religion,knowledge,psychology,p hilosophy........any trying to understand and follow it truely.Perhaps we have forgotten the Greatest Philosopher,and guru of Alexander/ Sikandar,asked him after conquering India,bring me Self Realised Soul,since they are only in India,and even at that time Maharishi*

*Matang did't bowed and finally refused Sikandar,and told him,he won't be able to reach Yunaan/Egypt..stay with him for three days,to save yourself.*

**Somnath Banerjee in reply to Rishi Ramesh Vishv...**
*East or west, destruction of family continues to be the cause of turmoil in the soul of human.*

*Crusader means a long and determined attempt to achieve something that you believe in strongly: Hinduism does not believe in crusades.*

**Rishi Ramesh Vishvas in reply to Somnath Banerjee**
*Sorry,we are still not able to rise above the denomination.HE sent us all as a soul,rest are the name of bodies,once we rise above it,can easily understand soul does't turmoil anybody,any relation.*

*Need to awake from the creations of mind.*

**Somnath Banerjee in reply to Rishi Ramesh Vishv...**

*An embodied soul is the sole enjoyer both pain and pleasure as per Gita. You have rightly said*

*"HE sent us all as a soul," so soul is also in turmoil. You can differ in your opinion.*

### 19. ARJUNA "S QUESTION NO 4- I REQUEST YOU TO TELL ME, DECISIVELY, WHAT IS BETTER FOR ME. I AM YOUR DISCIPLE. TEACH ME WHO HAS TAKEN REFUGE IN YOU. (2.07)

**Syed Amir**
*Constantly keep yourself headed in the right direction for you. It may not be easy at times, but in those times of struggle you will find a stronger sense of who you are.*

*So when the days come that are filled with frustration and unexpected responsibilities, remember to believe in yourself and all you want your life to be.*

*Because the challenges and changes will only help you to find the goals that you know are meant to come true for you.Keep Believing in Yourself!*

*Somnath Banerjee in reply to Syed Amir*
*You have brought out the success formula in Physical domain which is based on logic. But when emotions come in your intellect is cofused and your Ego gets shattered. It is at this stage you have to take help of some you love and respect/. Get to know yourself before you believe in yourself. Know what works best for you.*

*Sunil Kaisolagi*
*Nice article...*
*Somnath Banerjee in reply to Sunil Kaisolagi*
*thanks*

### 20. ARJUNA QUESTION -5- WHAT IS THE MARK OF A PERSON WHOSE PRAJNA IS STEADY AND MERGED IN SUPERCONSCIOUS STATE? HOW DOES A PERSON OF STEADY PRAJNA SPEAK? HOW DOES SUCH A PERSON SIT AND WALK? 2.54

*Anup Singh*
*Beautiful*

*Somnath Banerjee in reply to Anup Singh*
*Beauty lies in the eyes of beholder*

*Roli Pandey*
*Wonderful*

*Somnath Banerjee in reply to Roli Pandey*
43 *When is transcendental knowledge better than work? 2. To engage in this horrible war', Are not all war horrible? 3. Do modes of nature allow work without attachment? 4. Do transcendental knowledge have any reparations in the physical domain of human life. 5. Was Gandhari right in accusing Krishna for getting her 100 son killed. Please be free to express your views, so that we may understand Karma Yog better. Which question set you pondering*

*Somnath Banerjee in reply to Sandesh Saboo*
*'if You think that intelligence is better than fruitive work? '*

*You have used intelligence for transcendental Knowledge. Data of inner and outer world are are classified into attributes and function and stored as information, the neural network controller processes the information to gain intelligence, the intelligence is verified and validated to gain knowledge it may be stored in the EGO which may affect the soul.*

*"he wanted to skillfully avoid the fighting by using Krsna consciousness as an excuse. "*

*Arjuna is not offering any excuse for not fighting, here the war has not began.*

*You may like to explain role of transcendental knowledge and work in the three domains in which a man lives.*

### Somnath Banerjee in reply to Sandesh Saboo
*Just what is the Bhagavad-gita? The purpose of Bhagavad-gita is to deliver mankind from the nescience of material existence. Every man is in difficulty in so many ways, as Arjuna also was in difficulty in having to fight the Battle of Kuruksetra. Arjuna surrendered unto Sri Krsna, and consequently this Bhagavad-gita was spoken. Not only Arjuna, but every one of us is full of anxieties because of this material existence. Our very existence is in the atmosphere of nonexistence. Actually we are not meant to be threatened by nonexistence. Our existence is eternal. But somehow or other we are put into asat. Asat refers to that which does not exist.*

*The subject of the Bhagavad-gita entails the comprehension of five basic truths. First of all, the science of God is explained and then the constitutional position of the living entities, jivas. There is isvara, which means controller, and there are jivas, the living entities which are controlled. If a living entity says that he is not controlled but that he is free, then he is insane. The living being is controlled in every respect, at least in his conditioned life. So in the Bhagavad-gita the subject matter deals with the isvara, the supreme controller, and the jivas, the controlled living entities. Prakrti (material nature) and time (the duration of existence of the whole universe or the manifestation of material nature) and karma (activity) are also discussed. The cosmic manifestation is full of different activities. All living entities are engaged in different activities. From Bhagavad-gita we must learn what God is, what the living entities are, what prakrti is, what the cosmic manifestation is, how it is controlled by time, and what the activities of the living entities are.*

**His Divine Grace A.C. Bhaktivedanta Swami Prabhupada.**
*My own version I shall furnish if you desire*
*Somnath Banerjee in reply to Sandesh Saboo*
*What is dharma?*
*what is shetra of dharma?*
*what is kuruShetra?*

*very pertinent questions and answers showing your profound knowledge of Geeta..*

*I do not get bothered by context based dharmas as lord Krishna finally directed to shun all dharmasand surrender to him..*

*You have analyzed fields as per chapter 13 in details as I understand this body is field for the life force to operate. The functionality and attributes are the expectation value some manifested some unmanifested.,*

*Kurushetra is conflict in mental domain, generated by modes of nature in the mind.*

**Somnath Banerjee in reply to Sandesh Saboo**
*You have not understood surrender.*

*When you surrender all your action and reaction has to conform to the will of lord*

*You cannot commit sin.here in second line lord is promising to absolve all sins, sins committed before and after surrender. Ie karmic cycle stops*

### 21. Arjuna's Question No7
*You seem to confuse my mind by apparently conflicting words. Tell me, decisively, one thing by which I may attain the Supreme. (gita 3.2)*

**Debi Acharya**
*Knowledge with action lead to devotion entails surrender and salvation. Very true.*

*What good is knowledge if no action is taken? One needs to know the Brahman (Knowledge) and take action (Yoga, meditation, Japa Swadhyaya etc.) in order to achieve salvation.*

*Nothing happens of its own, what we want we must make that happen.*

**Sumita Kataria**
*Respected Sir*
*what is knowledge ?*
*kindly explain knowledge*
*with action*
*Ishwar hamesha saath hai*

**Swaran Omcawr**
*"One who sees the path of renunciation*

*And the path of work as the same, really sees. Both lead to the Supreme"- Holy Geeta*

*A great piece of wisdom! A highest ideal if ever for life!!*

*So that is why we should not leave the world of phenomenon, this whole mayajaal, this whole involvement in mundane affairs.*

*But at the same time must think of that pursuing worldly life only we shall be free from it.*

*And not by leaving the world.*
*or going into a life of escapism*
*escaping into woods,*
*institutionalized spirituality,*
*whole time affair of chewing of spiritual stuff,*
*or simply saying---*
*ADOPTING SANYAAS*

**Ravi Kiran**
*Knowledge with action... Yes, doer-ship based actions are absent in the case of one having Self Knowledge....*

**Somnath Banerjee in reply to Ravi Kiran**
*Not necessarily true*

**Ravi Kiran in reply to Somnath Banerjee**
*If so, its not right knowledge..*

**Somnath Banerjee in reply to Ravi Kiran**
*Are you referring to Buddha*

**Ravi Kiran in reply to Somnath Banerjee**
*No, just responding to the thread we were conversing on doer-ship based actions. ..*

**Somnath Banerjee in reply to Ravi Kiran**
*Knowledge and action going hand in hand*

**Ravi Kiran in reply to Somnath Banerjee**
*Yes, one who sees inaction in action, and action in inaction, while engaged in activities..*

**Somnath Banerjee in reply to Ravi Kiran**
*Two are not same.. My next blog Shall discuss inaction in action, and action in inaction,*

**Ravi Kiran in reply to Somnath Banerjee**
*Yes, they are not. ..the one who sees IS..*

**Somnath Banerjee in reply to Ravi Kiran**
*In this world there are two kinds of created beings. One is called the divine and the other demoniac. '*

*Knowledge and action are applicable to both.*

*Absence of doership when one transcends the modes of nature in case of Dinive beings.*

*while it is not so in case of andrake people*

**Ravi Kiran in reply to Somnath Banerjee**
*Yes, its primarily having to do with presence of Self Knowledge or Ignorance(avidya). ..Once identified with ignorance, it can take any shape or force, causing self destruction and destruction of world. ..On the other, one with Self Knowledge is a True Blessing to creation...*

**Somnath Banerjee in reply to Ravi Kiran**
*Vishnu says curse of Kumaras cannot be reversed. Instead, he gives Jaya and Vijaya two options. The first option is to take seven births on Earth as a devotee of Vishnu, while the second is to take three births as his enemy. After serving either of these sentences, they can re-attain their stature at Vaikuntha and be with him permanently. Jaya and Vijaya cannot bear the thought of staying away from Vishnu for seven lives. As a result, they choose to be born three times on Earth even though it would have to be as enemies of Vishnu.*

*The story reveal that you gain freedom from death and life cycle faster when endowed with demoniacal soul. Reconcile*

### Rati Hegde in reply to Somnath Banerjee
*Sir i am not an expert but i think that your last para is incorrect. The 3 lives of Jaya and Vijaya lasted for a longer time than an average life which spanned 7 births. Even if you believed in the stories as it is, then too your last para is incorrect.*

### Somnath Banerjee in reply to Rati Hegde
*You have commented on my blog for the first time, so i will not bring out the fallacies of your comment.*
*now appreciate*
*a divine soul has to transcend the three Gunas and then surrender.*
*both have chances to fail as lords Maya is very powerful*
*a demoniacal soul is enemy of lord, lord incarnates to kill them and offer salvation.*
*see bible ' killing the serpent by Mary*

### Ravi Kiran in reply to Somnath Banerjee
*Bhakt Prahlad, though born in Asuras family, was endowed with such devotion arising from Self Knowledge, was never separated from Maha Vishnu..the story reveals that by knowing one's True Nature, one experiences freedom here and now..*

### Somnath Banerjee in reply to Ravi Kiran
*KNOWLEDGE of self is the key to the knowledge of God, according to the saying: "He who knows himself knows God," and, as it is Written in the Koran, "We will show them Our signs in the world and in themselves, that the truth may be manifest to them."*

*The idea of the highest passion of subjectivity is towards self-knowledge. As per Budhism*

*self knowledge leads to Nirvana.*

*Both divine and demons are endowed with Self Knowledge, both can reach supreme.*

### Ravi Kiran in reply to Somnath Banerjee
*Yes, KNOWLEDGE of self is the key..*

### Somnath Banerjee in reply to Ravi Kiran
*Action and devotion cannot be belittled*

**Ravi Kiran in reply to Somnath Banerjee**
*True, each has its significance..*

**Somnath Banerjee in reply to Ravi Kiran**
*Follow gita- knowledge- action-devotion- surrender- salvation.*

**Ravi Kiran in reply to Somnath Banerjee**
*One in All and All in One*

**Somnath Banerjee in reply to Ravi Kiran**
*It was one of my blog.*
*diversity of nature is creation of your mind*
*knower of truth do not get deluded.*

**Ravi Kiran in reply to Somnath Banerjee**
*True*

**Somnath Banerjee in reply to Ravi Kiran**
*Welcome*

**Cosmic Entity in reply to Somnath Banerjee**
*"the story reveal that you gain f faster when endowed with demoniacal soul."*

*What type of logic / explanation is this? Going by this the people who are looking for the ultimate freedom should become demonic. Hitler might have got the "freedom from death and life cycle" by now, Osama Bin Laden must be in the line !*

*These are mythological stories only written to convey a different message to humanity. Unfortunately people take these stories as real incidents and forget to apply the learning in their life.*

*This mythology and religion has ruined this country (my opinion !)*

**Somnath Banerjee in reply to Cosmic Entity**
*What type of logic / explanation is this?*
*Divine souls see lord as friend and demoniacal soul see lord as enemy*
*friends you may forget but enemies you cannot, they always remember him*
*any one remembering him at the time of death(gita ch 4) is provided salvation.*

**Cosmic Entity in reply to Somnath Banerjee**
*Yet another apologetic reasoning !*
*Fine Sir.*
*Thank you* ☺

**Somnath Banerjee in reply to Cosmic Entity**
*Salvation*

*Islam*
*1. To testify that none has the right to be worshipped but Allah and Muhammad is Allah's Apostle.*
*2. To offer the compulsory prayers dutifully and perfectly.*
*3. To pay Zakat to poor and needy (i.e. obligatory charity of 2.5% annually of surplus wealth).*
*4. To perform Hajj. (i.e. Pilgrimage to Mecca)*
*5. To observe fast during the month of Ramadhan. Sahih al-Bukhari, 1:2:7*
*Performing the mandatory acts of worship, Muslims have the chance of salvation*

*Buddhaism*
*No God or gods. Salvation is not related to Buddhism at all. The Buddha also told us to depend on our own to attain nirvana (by dominant the Threefold Training or the Eightfold path..*

*Christanity*
*Only God is good and therefore only God is able to save a person. Jesus came down from Heaven to save mankind. Follow the The ten commandment and salvation is guaranteed*

**Cosmic Entity in reply to Somnath Banerjee**
*Sir,*

*Who has got the salvation or the Moksha till date? No one can prove that. There are no salvation or moksha happening. If you believe in Atman or soul stuff then understand this point that you, me and others are present here since the very beginning of the creation (assuming it happened as mentioned in scriptures). Just follow the simple logic. You are here which mean you have not attain salvation. For you to exist today, you must be having a previous life, this is Simple Karma logic. For you to have a previous life you got to have a previous to previous life. Just keep on going back this way you will soon realize you have been present since the very beginning ! There is no salvation no moksha. No one can with the guarantee that the children born tomorrow is not the current them.*

*And Sir going by the Hindu scriptures this is the story of current instance of the Universe which has a life span of 311 Trillion solar years (equals 100 years of Brahma). The current Age of the Universe is 155 Trillion years. I had read it somewhere that till date many Brahma have died.*

*It's going on since eternity and will never stop otherwise the need of God to exist will cease.*

*People may find this logic weird or stupid, but it is fine to me.*

*Thanks and Regards* ☺

### Somnath Banerjee in reply to Cosmic Entity
*Your logic is neither weird or stupid. What you have concluded is fundamental of all religion that your mortal body dies but life is immortal.*

*Now salvation as i have highlighted various modes of salvation, it seems there is a comonility*
*to control lust,greed and anger.*
*you get salvation from what ? sin.*
*Where is sin? It is in the mind.*
*can you wipe out sin? You have to clean the mind*
*can you clean the mind? Yes – you have gained salvation.*
*please note salvation has nothing to do with GOD.*

### Cosmic Entity in reply to Somnath Banerjee
*Sir,*

*If the religions do not tell this type of stuff who is going to follow them? Humans are worried all the time about their future and find comfort if someone elder tell them every thing will be fine. If the same is said by peer or younger person psychologically it does not make impact. Every person understand that this world, this universe is not created by humans so it is easy to fit the idea that only God could have done it.*

*Our brain can be fooled easily. When people start justifying their wrong / irrational actions on the lines of religious teachings then it becomes apologetic. But it is still tricky as "wrong action" is subjective.*

*I am not against Hinduism only. To me every religion is more or less the same with the same goal of making the fool out of common people.*

*As a personal choice I rate Buddhism above any other religion. Oldness of religion is not a deciding factor whether a certain religion make sense, or the most correct religion. This is very much applicable to the followers of Hinduism.*

*I don't know if I am making any sense to you. One last thing, Human Brain is the biggest delusion generator and a belief engine we know of as of now. It will accept any belief that help us to go through the day smoothly and it does not matter how stupid or irrational those beliefs may be !*

*Thank you and Regards* ☺

**Somnath Banerjee in reply to Cosmic Entity**
*You are God of your World see my blog.*
*my conclusions are similar to you.*

**Cikkvsarkfiyt Lihsajyrv in reply to Somnath Banerjee**
*To kya kare O_o*

**Somnath Banerjee in reply to Cikkvsarkfiyt Lihs...**
*You think you are the doer!*

**Cikkvsarkfiyt Lihsajyrv in reply to Somnath Banerjee**
*Nahi to kya :P i m typing :D*

**Somnath Banerjee in reply to Cikkvsarkfiyt Lihs...**
*I could not decipher*

**Cikkvsarkfiyt Lihsajyrv in reply to Somnath Banerjee**
*Mene kah amei hi to TYPE kar rha hu. . to DOER kon hua :P*

**Somnath Banerjee in reply to Cikkvsarkfiyt Lihs...**
*Yes you are the doer.*
*but who are you?*
*your eyes see. When you die eyes cannot see. You are not there. Similarly all action.*
*from sensing to action is not deterministic process but stochastic. Ponder*

**Cikkvsarkfiyt Lihsajyrv in reply to Somnath Banerjee**
*Okay* ☺

**Somnath Banerjee in reply to Cikkvsarkfiyt Lihs...**
*Welcome*

**Cikkvsarkfiyt Lihsajyrv**
*Kaha\**

**Somnath Banerjee in reply to Cikkvsarkfiyt Lihs...**
*What is it, i am weak in hindi*

**Cikkvsarkfiyt Lihsajyrv in reply to Somnath Banerjee**
*Nothing it was improvement of typo error of my previous comment*
*Reply*

**Somnath Banerjee in reply to Cikkvsarkfiyt Lihs...**
*Ok*

**Tanish Singh Slathia**
*The essence and lessons of life are contained in Gita*

**Somnath Banerjee in reply to Tanish Singh Slat...**
*You are correct. But life is yours. Enjoy pain and pleasure.*

**Somnath Banerjee in reply to Tanish Singh Slat...**
*We are discussing one question at a time,*
*please do comment in particular and not in general*

## 23. REINCARNATION

**Cikkvsarkfiyt Lihsajyrv**
*Mujhe to reinc. Ka topic bhut boring lagta hai !*

**Somnath Banerjee in reply to Cikkvsarkfiyt Lihs...**
*Lost in causelessness of life.*

**Sajal Gupta**
*Very nice blog*

**Somnath Banerjee in reply to Sajal Gupta**

*thanks*

**G S Chawla**
*A blog on reincarnation is thought provoking 'Human is the highest creation Of Almighty ! God ! ' & it is mortal & it is certain, but soul*

*is immortal & part of God.(Divine Spark). "kaie janam bichhde the madhav,yeh janam tumhare lekhe" Our Good deeds or bad deeds effects on our living (past or Present). "AS you sow,So shall you reap." (If you Sow an apple tree,it is not expected to get banana,or mango). Where there Science ends, Spirituality starts. "Bhae prapt manukh de huria,Gobind andr ki eho teri baria" (SGGS). Western philosophy depends on Eat,Drink,& be merry.Only enjoy who has seen the next. This thought is effecting our young generation& spoiling their culture.& decreasing the respect.*

### Cosmic Entity in reply to Gs Chawla
*"'Human is the highest creation Of Almighty !"*

*What makes you say that? Are you absolutely sure that there is no other life form in the Universe other than what is found on Earth?*

*If yes then it is a very strange choice of your God that it created the species which is absolutely determined to destroy everything it can, including the species itself !*

*Thanks*

### Gs Chawla in reply to Cosmic Entity
*In eastern philosophy our seers, saints,Gurus,prophet has stated 84 lac jonis,in &on earth,water,air,sky,water etc. 'Human has a purpose of life' but they are social animals,their basic needs & motives are similar to animals,but being social they have to obey & follow the norms.All are not equal.Individual differences are there,Due to language& intelligence human can control other species,& can train them.But his eating habits are different according to Geographical conditions and availability of foods,Some are veg. Some are non veg.The purpose of life is to remember God & do good deeds for society and other creation in cosmos.But Human Ego & lust creates the problems.*

### Cosmic Entity in reply to Gs Chawla
*Sir,*

*Agreed our sages and scriptures have said that there are 8.4 million species but it is not a number that is carved in stone. The current scientific estimate says the number of species are in the rang of 8.5 – 9.0 million species. I am not sure whether the estimate includes the species that are already extinct but I think they do.*

*I cannot say the same about the numbers mentioned in our scriptures. If that number must remain constant, then where are the rest of the species? And what about type of species scientist are able to create in the labs and are not found in nature? For e.g Liger, a cross between a tiger and a lion or a cross between a donkey and a zebra?*

*What you are saying is more about culture, behavior, instincts, psychology etc.. Some of these are applicable to other species also (obviously not to the same extent)*

*Every species has one and only one purpose in life and that is to maintain the continuity of it's species, add to the knowledge already known and pass it down as a solid base for it's next generation. From time to time Nature takes a test of all the species in it's own ways. If any species fails to pass the test it is eliminated over a period of time. Humans are extremely adaptable in almost all type of situation and that is why we are at the top of the food chain.*

*Unfortunately the growing human population and our greed has put a lot of pressure on the echosystem and has accelerated the eleminataion process of other species.*

*When nature eliminates it knows how to maintain the balance but humans riding on their ego trip, do not.*

*The God thing is all human made. Just give it a thought that why would God create a species that is determined to destroy his other creation as well as the self itself? Is this the case that the omniscient God did not knew what it's creation going to do in future. From the type of powers people associate with God, it is not possible that he didn't knew? The defenders of the faith might say that it is not possible to understand the "leela of the God" by ordinary humans. This type of reasoning is nothing but an apologetic response by the defenders of the faith !*

*Thank you.*

**Somnath Banerjee in reply to Cosmic Entity**
*You are not appreciating why man made God*

**Cosmic Entity in reply to Somnath Banerjee**
*Sir,*
*By mistake I end up deleting my previous comment sorry for that..*

*"You are not appreciating why man made God"*

*I am not clear about what you meant by the above statement*

*Do you wish to know why man created God? Something else, can you please clarify?*

*Thank you*

**Somnath Banerjee in reply to Cosmic Entity**
*Forces of nature(Gods) created man with consciousness and free will. Then man created god to blame or credit him for his present state*

**Cosmic Entity in reply to Somnath Banerjee**
*Sir,*

*I think we should keep Nature (Gods) away from this discussion. And please also note that I equate Nature with God (my problem). Nature contribution is implicit and cannot be ignored. All the raw material has come the nature itself.*

*Consider this, In nature there are 92 elements, however human have gone on to create additional 28 elements and thus the element count is 120. Yes the raw material was provided by nature but nature has not created them directly. Similarly human are not created by nature directly.*

*Human existence is very mysterious.*

*Consciousness again is again tricky. There is no Universal Consciousness, There is only Energy and Energy is not conscious on it's own. Also inorganic matter doesn't have any consciousness whatsoever. I think consciousness is not a thing but an ever evolving process that links our mind, brain, thoughts and memories and the ecosystem together and gives us a subjective experience of the objective reality.*

*Free Will is another tricky subject. Is there is free will, well I am more towards not side, even if we have, it is very restricted (the neurons in the brain will fire when they need to, not when we want to ) People says we have "Free Will" and give an example that I can raise my hand any time, because of my free will. But it is not true. We only explain things consciously. By the time we are thinking about raising the hand, the event has already happened. This is the reason that our actions can be captured anywhere between 8 to 10 second before they enter our our conscious mind and decoded successfully with high degree of accuracy (all thoughts originate in our unconscious mind)*

*This is my limited understanding, there are lots of things which are unexplainable as of now. By saying there is no Free Will, I am in no way implying that our lives are predetermined*

*Feel free to dismiss it, if it doesn't make sense ;-D I can only ask you to do that and won't try to convince you.*

*Regards* ☺

### Somnath Banerjee in reply to Cosmic Entity

*When life function operates on the energy system of the brain Consciousness emerges, your space and time starts. . interaction of consciousness takes place creating an illusion of Universal consciousness,free will*

*A belief in free will touches nearly everything that human beings value. It is difficult to think about law, politics, religion, public policy, intimate relationships, morality – as well as feelings of remorse or personal achievement – without first imagining that every person is the true source of his or her thoughts and actions. And yet the facts tell us that free will is an illusion.*

### Cosmic Entity in reply to Somnath Banerjee
*Sir,*

*In a way I am on the right track then. You said "your space and time starts" that is what subjective experience of objective reality"*

*"without first imagining that every person is the true source of his or her thoughts and actions. And yet the facts tell us that free will is an illusion"*

*Every thoughts, emotions and actions start in our Unconscious Mind. Which seems to say that it has to be our free will because of which they are generating in our unconscious mind, probably that is why many people think we have "free will". What is missing here is (as per my understanding) what causes these thoughts, emotions and action to originate in the first place. Some researches says this happens due to the physics of the Universe (laws of nature) and it is difficult to understand that if I wish to eat an apple, how the physics of the Universe is acting behind the scene to create a thought in my unconscious mind.*

*Please let me know if you have some information on this.*

*There is another type of "no free will" argument and it usually comes from the hardcore believers. They say that nothing happens without the grace of God, from smallest to the largest event one can think of. Every second of our life is predetermined etc.. I do not support this type of argument at all. What is your opinion on this?*

*I read somewhere (out of context)*

*"We are connected to each other Biologically, to the Earth Chemically and to the Universe Atomically"*

*Thank you*

**Somnath Banerjee in reply to Cosmic Entity**
*you have put lot of effort on understanding free will.our brain is complex in functioning. It has a operating system called mind, It is multiple input and multiple output system. It also learns.If you appreciate neural network. The output depends on aggregation of multiple weighted inputs through a transfer function with hidden layers. The outputs are not same for the same input. An artificial intelligence of minimum 11 dimension resemble our brain which is free will.*

**Cosmic Entity in reply to Somnath Banerjee**
*Thank you Sir for appreciating my efforts ;)*

*Mind is an operating system of our brain. It is said that anywhere between 95-99% of our lives are run by our "unconscious mind". This whole spiritual quest seems to be about shifting the control from our "unconscious mind" to our "conscious mind".*

*Neural Networks are at core of every Artificial Intelligence (AI) System. The initial phases are all about leaning it is similar to what happens in the brain once we are born. New connections are formed, re-assigned and the older connections are cut. Once the connections are stabilized then only real learning happens and it continues till we are dead.*

*Check this out -*
*The Human Brain Project*
*https://www.humanbrainproject.eu/*
*The Blue Brain Project*
*http://www.artificialbrains.com/blue-brain-project*

*Both are aimed at understanding the complete human brain functionality from the scratch.*

*"an artificial intelligence of minimum 11 dimension resemble our brain which is free will"*

*Interesting ! 11 dimensions are used in String / M-Theory. Is our "free will" somehow related to String / M-Theory?*

*Thanks* ☺

**Somnath Banerjee in reply to Gs Chawla**
*I must submit that law of causation i.e Cause & effect is applicable in the physical domain and partially in mental domain and the process is stochastic in spiritual domain.*

*but looking into immortality of life some correlation with cause and effect.*

**Gs Chawla in reply to Somnath Banerjee**
*VERY TRUE, WELCOME YOUR VIEWS.GOD IS IMMORTAL AS WELL AS THE SOUL,WE should rise from bodily needs. Spirituality leads towards Divine powers.Ultimately soul has to merge with Almighty! As a drop of water has to merge with a vast ocean..*

**Somnath Banerjee in reply to Gs Chawla**
*Budist believe in reincarnation although it does not believe in God. you may answer my four questions without andrake to God*

**Cosmic Entity in reply to Somnath Banerjee**
*Sir,*

*There are three extremely long threads on Reincarnation by Pramila Ji (Pramila Davidson). I request you to have a look at them. Probably you will find many more answers.*

*There is a difference in Hindu Reincarnation and Buddhist Reincarnation. And there is usage of another word named "Rebirth". You will find almost everything in those three threads. Thank you.*

**Somnath Banerjee in reply to Cosmic Entity**
*How are you cosmic? Long time no see. Pramilaji is quoting findings of third party,hence you have to discount information content.*
*the andrake and buddhaism explain reincarnation on the basis of karmic theory.. whether you set ten levels or thousand level it does not matter because life is a stochastic process*

**Cosmic Entity in reply to Somnath Banerjee**
*Hello Sir,*

*I am currently in a 50-50 state (neither too good nor too bad) ;-D. I hope you are doing good. I was absent for three months, got bored with ST.*

*"Pramilaji is quoting findings of third party,hence you have to discount information content."*

*As you wish Sir, actually I had written. Actually I had written many comment about the belief in reincarnation.*

*"andrake and buddhaism explain reincarnation on the basis of karmic theory."*

*The most important difference between a Hindu reincarnation and Buddhist reincarnation is that Buddhism does not believe in Soul / Atma / Self. They believe in the concept of "No Self". They do not even believe even in Hindu Brahman. To them there is not creation, the universe is eternal.*

*Atman / Soul / Self and Brahman are the core pillars on which Hinduism stands. The difference in the core concept of any religion(s) indicates that all religion are man made including the scriptures, otherwise there cannot be so much difference about core concepts*

*"whether you set ten levels or thousand level it does not matter because life is a stochastic process"*

*Life is a process? Yes from my side, can't say about others. After quite sometime I came across a person who see life as process :-D*

*I did not understand how it is a "stochastic process"*

*Stochastic means random process, right? So I would like to know if you have used it for random process or something else. If not then please elaborate your comment.*

*Thank you ;)*

**Somnath Banerjee in reply to Cosmic Entity**
*A random process has two parts 1 random variable and its distribution. The random variable are created from outcome of an event and is time determinant however its distribution is stationary. When the random process has a distribution which varies with time it is called stochastic process.*

*Eg, DNA of man and woman unite to produce offspring having different DNA.*

*Each sperm has life (say 50000) attack an egg. Which sperm will fertilize nobody knows.*

*DNA has 23 pair of chromosomes, how these 46 pair shall produce new ones you are unable to predict. Life is stochastic process.*

**Gs Chawla in reply to Somnath Banerjee**
*Whether Believer or non believer of God ! but some power is there to control the things 24/7 all the time.There was a camp of Budhist at Bangalore,10days back,they all were from different parts of the country & some from other Nations.(Followers of H.H.DalaiLama.).I was one of the speaker on andrak.,God ! purpose of Life, Ego & Salvation.1). Can you see ? the air,fragrance,current,fire in the wood,Not visible but it is there.Same case with the God,2). Human is the highest creation of God! & he is a mortal only Almighty! God is immortal. Our soul is also immortal.3).As the clouds covers the Sun & moon.sometime it is not visible.Due to our Ego& illusion we cannot realize The God ! that within us all. We have to realize it by grace of the true Guru or God Himself.4). Human body perishes but soul not,it changes the body or merge in Divine power as the drop of water merges with vast ocean.we say incarnation.We see many types of animals, birds,creatures on the earth & water,sky etc.Man is a social animal because he lives in society.Life is circle like water,rain,sea,sun.Approximately 84lacs jonis.human is the highest creation on this earth ultimately he has to get salvation remembering the Divine power,you can give any name,God,Gravity,Ram,Gopal,Gobind,Hari,Allah,Thaku r.etc.etc.*

**Somnath Banerjee in reply to Gs Chawla**
*Very Knowledgeable response. 'God ! purpose of Life, Ego & Salvation.' Is interesting.*

*You have correlated immortality of soul with reincarnation.you may appreciate*
*1 evolution of life in 8000km dia rock.*
*2 interaction of life with life*
*3 cleansing of soul*
*4 life and divine spark are not different.*

**Gs Chawla in reply to Somnath Banerjee**
*WELCOME YOUR VIEWS.*

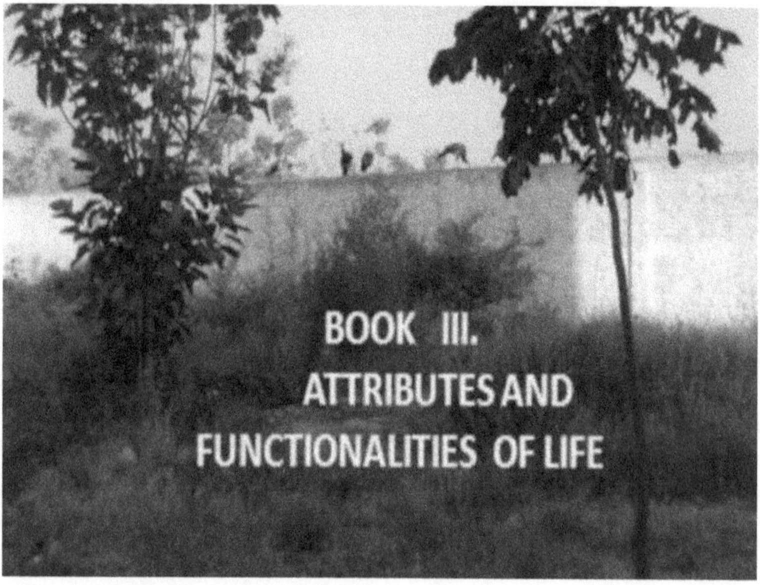
BOOK III.
ATTRIBUTES AND
FUNCTIONALITIES OF LIFE

# BOOK III.
## ATTRIBUTES AND FUNCTIONALITIES OF LIFE

## COMMENTS

# 24. NOTHING NEW ONLY GRADUAL EVOLUTION

Saga of lust, greed and anger
Why worry it is everywhere.
 New sun, or new moon
Modification is not seen

Students come and go
Evolutions in syllabus continue
 Life begin or life ends
Living change marginally
Love begins or love ends
Life continues shamelessly

Glory to nascent life
Each moment new strive.
There is nothing new only gradual evolution
There may be few opposing this proposition
Nature has endowed you with a form factor
everything change but for this vital vector

# 25. SO WHAT IF I AM A BUBBLE

So what if I am a bubble in the infinite ocean of consciousness.
So what if I am less stronger than many species of the universe,
So what if my name and fame do not compare with other bubbles
So what if my senses are less keen and have not spotted trouble.
So what if I am yet to win laurels in any life threatening scuffle
So what if I have failed in game of life, no one has got out alive.

I know that I am highest creation, I have inherited all the traits
Accumulated over eons, with algorithms of nature in built in me.
I am the creator of my world, the physical world around me
I see what I want to see and I hear what I want to hear.
 I enjoy pain and pleasure, my body is finest piece of art
I grow and adjust to ambience, I generate power of my own.
I eat food and metabolize them, I can sense and act effectively.
But most important I have superior intelligence and free will.

I am fully self healing system, I interact and reproduce
I control nature and dominate over other species.
When my bubble burst, I shall be one with the ocean
My body shall disintegrate and return to elements.

My ever inquisitive mind cannot fathom this ocean
Though I have distributed neural network
With central processing unit called brain.
The attributes and functions distributed spatially
Creating my world which surely is mine own
This is my mind operating in mental domain.

I can fault find and repair any part by thinking only.
I am aware of configuration and my performance
I have built in security, flight or fight for survival
So what if I am a bubble in the ocean of consciousness.

My space and time commences at my manifestation
I am hero of my life, I am God of my world.
Five billion manifestation is crowding this globe
Some live or die but immortality of life need no probe

*Comments attached*

# 26. CARAVAN OF LIFE PASS BY SWIFTLY

Caravan of life pass by swiftly
Raising curtains of ambiguity
Childhood in guileless splendour
Youth in defenseless infatuation
Roasted in fire of love and affection
Fire is now lost but memory lingers.
Collecting moving chromed steel boxes
Fabricating brick walls for security
Accumulating wealth loosing health
Is story of every upward mobile person.

Meaningful relationship remains sacrificed
Tea and coffee is consumed in gallons
Every available moment spent on
To get something more, yes more.

Parents are sacrificed for lack of time
Wife is lost due to superficial life
Children go astray due to low care
Self is butchered in daily stress and strain.

Whole life you only take like a thief
End has neared, why now turn to Belief.
 But Lord is kind full of grace and mercy
With his help I shall surely save my face

I have acted as per modes of nature
That You have endowed in my care
If I am sinner you are also sinner
With this realization, I have no fear

Time is nearing to leave this world facade
I shall be accepted in your abode with grace

# 27. CHANGING HUES OF MY LIFE

Biting cold of winter is no more
 Burning heat of summer yet to gore
Sun rises red turning pink then golden
 Nature lay blushing like a fair maiden.
Full of bloom of multifaceted hues
 Birds and bees hover drinking dews
 All beasts are out of hibernation
Calling mates for frolic in unison.
Celebration of spring is in full swing
With colors and sweets market is flushing
Age, race and gender are no more barrier
 Coloring each other obliterating exterior

Many a hue in my life I have donned
 Some colored me blue some green
Fiery red of youth has now withered
Now only black and white is seen
Thirteen summers in blue black shorts
Twenty six summers in olive green
 Last score in white shirt and black suit
Unchanged was my light brown sheet
Coloring and embracing is continuing
More as spectator than player enjoying
 Intensity of physical calisthenic is ebbing
 Deficiency in self knowledge is revealing
My multi hued thoughts are slowly abetting
With equanimity incognito face is glowing.
 My fission mind sought solace in fusion
I have lost myself in Your colorful vision.

# 28. FACTS OF LIFE

Fight is for life but
Death is inevitable.
Reality never cease to exist yet
Existence is time dependent function.
All the cycles studied in this universe
Cannot explain life and death cycle.
Nothing is static everything is dynamic yet
Dynamics is static at any instant of time.
In spite of logic, emotion always hold sway
In all human knowledge ignorance's fray.
So surrender to the life force
That controls you and your destiny
Paradox of life I am yet to fathom
When it starts or ends nobody knows
If you are certain of anything in life,
Please do convey, it would be nice
Yet we hold this transient entity dearly
Survival is inbuilt in us, fight or flight
All your logic and emotion fail
When your survival is at stake.
You are main hero of your life
When it ends you are history.
You are god of your world
Your honour and dignity depends on it
This world is embedded in mental perception
You are seeking it, within and without, with perspiration
Duality is inbuilt in your life function
Virtues and vices are present at every junction.
Everyone has his own success story
Desires his progeny to do better than him.
You are to ensure immortality of life
Let no one misguide you to do otherwise
There is no escape from life and death cycle
All talk of salvation are bogus mumble
To every man his own madness
His salvation lies in its success.

# 29 LIFE AND MIND (MUNDRAKE UPANISHAD)

life is considered a characteristic of something that exhibits Homeostasis, Organization Metabolism, Growth Adaptation, Response to stimuli and Reproduction. When that something is human it is very complex, Human are intelligent and has free will the hardware for these is the brain with its extensive neural network. The brain has more than billion neurons. The neurons are distributed in multiple brain complexes. the brain is supported by many energy centers (glands) which carry out specific functions, the algorithm with which it is controlled is called mind A mind is the set of cognitive faculties that enables consciousness, perception, thinking, judgment, and memory—a characteristic of humans..

Life has two components like any Energy vector–one kinetic other potential vector. The kinetic element interacts with five physical elements and three mental elements and establishes the mind which is a set of cognitive faculties that enables consciousness, perception, thinking, judgment, and memory.

Man with physical features, active mental faculties under the influence of kinetic life element, is intelligent and has free will. Kinetic vector of life takes part in every decision of mind passively and manifests in human life as voice of conscience. Presumed to be located at pre frontal cortex complex...

The modes of nature starts dominating his life leads to miseries (bondage) due to mismatch of consciousness and conscience. Mind is not synchronous with life. Suggestion of voice of conscience being vetoed by Ego most of the time.

The static Energy vector of life is spectator to the functioning of mind and Kinetic life yet it is radiant and in bliss resting in the pineal gland controlling the consciousness.

When the human synchronies mind with kinetic life and observe the static life

His griefs are ended. He gains freedom.

Mundrake Upanishad states. || 3.1.01 ||3.1.2

Two birds of a feather, both nestling together, bearing same name, same cause to be, both clinging on to the same tree, one relishing fruits in lay happiness, the other looks on in bliss, mere witness On the same tree man sits grieving, drowned (in sorrow), bewildered, feeling helpless, But when he sees the other *Isa* (lord) content, knows his glory, his grief passes away.

Somnath S Banerjee Aapni chetna ke bal boote jab aadmi koi sidhant leta hai jo aapni jamir se nehi milti hai to dukhi ho jata hai. Lekin jab jamir aur chetna dono milker sidhant per pouchta hai to mun shant ho jata hai or dhukh vool jata hai.

# 30.LIFE IS INTOXICANT

Jaundice eyes can see only yellow
A craze clings, stays with the fellow
some are crazy for gaining knowledge
Some are mad about creative venture
Some are drunk for more power and position
 Some work ceaselessly to amass unlimited wealth
Some sweat-out daily to acquire physical strength.
All give you high briefly but hangover continues

Any one craze is sufficient for a lifetime
Though all your body cells gets change with time
Image created in your mind remains unchanged
Life is good or bad thinking makes it so.
Physical, social and financial barriers reduce the craze
Safety, security and volition needs try to make you sage
There are many barriers that douse the flame of rage
They deter you but it is your life and it is your gauge.
What is more hilarious than spending the life drunk
 In spite of bludgeoning of fate you do not feel pain
When there is failure, quite a number of them
Being intoxicated you do not feel any heartache.
 When someone cheats you of your dues and rights
You just smile, feeling sad for their short sight
There are tigers ready to chew you to pieces
There are snakes hissing up to poison you
There are bears jumping to hug you to death
All of them are in the garb of human being.
What can be more funny when you know others thought
Give them credit for their hypocrisy, you are a happy man
 Ready to help if you can, feel sad if you can not.
 Life is high grade intoxicant enjoy it slowly and surely.

*Comments attached*

# 31. HUMAN LIFE

Life is manifestation of life functions beginning in birth and terminating in death. Life interacts with energy system of the brain and consciousness begins to take shape. Your space and time starts now.

Your senses starts interacting with external world. Your inner world endowed in the brain complexes - mind, intellect and ego are working overtime to adjust to new environment.

Environment comprises sense objects, your senses are gratified with them and you develop attachment. It can be attractive or repulsive.

This attachment is central to interaction of consciousness. All your action and emotion are due to this attachment. There is no pain or pleasure once you are detached. You still bleed when you get cut but pain is below threshold of withstanding it.

From attachment springs desire. two things can happen

1.  Desire fulfilled may be after some striving – you get peace.

2.  Desire not fulfilled – results in anger, desire still persists then it is infatuation. In infatuation there is confusion of memory, loss of reason and leads to your ruin.

All logic and emotions are real when you are at it and appears delusion when you are out of it. In electricity we learn about two types Of current- one DC direct current and the other AC alternating current. Example of AC current is power supply from Power station whereas example of DC is Battery in mobile car etc. in DC voltage associated with current does not change with time or load whereas in AC voltage varies from positive crest to negative trough. An electric pulse is mixture of AC and DC and exist for small length of time.

Why am I talking about electric pulses?

The electro- chemical reaction in nervous system or neural network give rise to an electric pulse which is transported to brain. The mentro- nervo waves or thought is generated by these pulses. Under guidance of cortex various brain complexes take part and these are time integrated or rejected resulting in logic emotion and action.

Since AC at any instant is DC. All logic, emotion and action are not time invariant and are considered illusion or delusion they are all real at that phase of time.

Every human life perishes but life is immortal so life is truth. So are its ingredient, Female form in the west is considered truth and phallic symbol in the east is considered truth.

## 32. REALITIES OF LIFE (KORAN)

Realities of life as per Quran are presented for your comment

1.  Man and universe mismatch.
2.  Life divided in two parts
    a.  pre death period - life in the world
    b.  post death period – life in paradise.
3.  The real aim of creation is to select those who are fit for world of paradice. Paradise where creation like man attains complete fulfillment of desire..
4.  Criteria to qualify for Paradise
    a.  Acknowledge truth of One god and Surrender to him
    b.  live principled life- develop divine qualities.
5.  Right approach to creation plan
6.  The most important issue
    To be called into account before god. Every success gained in lifetime is trivial and mundane
7.  Gods imperatives through his prophets 'worship me.fulfil your obligation to another and live according to my will. I will punish those who fail to do this is a way that cannot be imagined.
8.  Death is a reality that everyone acknowledge.
9.  Life after death
10. The fact that the word man refers, not to any form but rather to the soul which inhibits the body.
11. Life and death to be accumulation and then subsequent diffusionof multitudinous particle of matter. Not true.It is made of atoms and life, when a man dies atoms remain but life departs.
12. How will I be judged
13  What is after world
14  Concept of accountability.
15  Man realize the realities,
Dear seekers how far are they real? please do comment

*Comments attached*

# 33. LIFE IS CREATIVE TILL TERMINATION

Lived frugally for sixty summers
Seems I have developed a habit of it
Minimum wants and maximum profit.
Profit does not thrill me anymore.
Valued Discipline and punctuality
remaining sincere and hardworking
Looking for more pay and promotion.
Promotion I don't strive anymore.
Strained myself physically and mentally
keeping my performance next to none
more degrees and positions ensued.
Performance I am not crazy anymore.
Some time ago I loved fun and frolic
Beauties and brains were my mates
I was loved and regarded by all.
Fun I don't dream of it anymore.
I loved and respected my family
Spending quality time I could afford
Facing separation I pined helplessly.
Family does not bond me anymore.
Festivals would enthuse fresh action
Many a fountain of fire have I negotiated
in my effort to gather benign attention.
Festivals don't fetch reaction anymore.
Friends of school were lost in college
College friends were lost in university
Transferable job scattered friendship.
Friendship does not entice anymore
Life lingeringly demand introspection
Why am I like this and not like that
Who is my role model or benchmark
Introspection does not lead me anywhere.
But craving for unbounded adventure has
Led to accelerated degradation of life function.
With diseased body, mind does not function
yet life is creative and meaningful till termination

## 34. ONLY TWO THINGS OF LIFE

You have only two things
One is your consciousness
And the other if your conscience
Consciousness function in your mind
Conscience is by product of your life,
Mismatching of mind and life leads to
confrontation and disharmony
Mind surrendering to life leads to bliss.
Divine consciousness conquered the forces of evil.
Enlighten your awareness to subdue your big ego.
All the pomp and show
 All the sweets consumption.
 All social interactions
Are collateral functions.
Consciousness and conscience are in confrontation
Your ego plays supreme in each and every interaction.
 Consciousness and conscience are in consensus
Victory is ensured in physical, mental and spiritual sphere.

*Comments attached*

# 35. CHANGELESSNESS

Only changeless is the change.
You are part of the change.
Change is implicit function of time
Changeless is the spectrum of life

Change can be gradual
Change can be incremental
Change can be cyclic
Change can be permanent.

You are restlessly searching for rest
Life dedicated for pursuit of happiness
Battle of life achieve peace at the end
Prosperity always waxes and wanes.

Life continues from synthesis to chaos,
Chaos to synthesis is always hidden
Overall spectrum remains the same
Whether you are in it or out of the game

Religion assures you changeless after life
You crave changelessness during Life. -
You may pray or bark or bray
Your hairs shall always turn grey.

## 36. DETACHMENT FROM THE WORLD

What would be the biggest obstacle to Self-realization? Deluded mind. The mind which is colored by our ego, attachment and desire. So detachment is the hardest part for our Self-realization? Yes, it's the hardest. The first step is removing attachment. The second step is it will weaken worldly desires. When attachment and desire are controlled, the ego will have no self-expression in the world.

What Is Attachment? In order for there to be attachment, you need two things -- the attacher, and the thing to which the attacher is attached. In other words, "attachment" requires self-reference, and it requires seeing the object of attachment as separate from oneself. Because we think we have intrinsic existence within our skin, and what's outside our skin is "everything else," that we go through life grabbing for one thing after another to make us feel safe, or to make us happy.

To achieve self realisation, happiness, inner peace, success, good relationships, and God-realization we must let go of all attachments and addictions. As Buddha said, "All suffering comes from attachment to ego cravings." That which we try to hold onto we lose. We may go too far and become totally detached, with no preferences. This is not good, either for then we are not involved in life. It is important to have a total passion for life and for all our goals, preference, and priorities, but the key is to be happy and have inner peace regardless of what happens. We shouldn't fight life.

He who binds to himself to Joy,
Does the winged life destroy;
 He who kisses the Joy as it flies,
Lives in Eternity's sunrise.
WILLIAM BLAKE

*Comments attached*

# 37. EVIDENCE OF PASSION AND DELUSION

Evidence of passion and delusion
I present to you for evaluation.
We have lived like self centered being
Yet cautious of what others are seeing.
Battle of life is reaching conclusion
Time has come for reorganization.
We have covered ground we cannot hold
Strength of beauty and brain is on hold.
There is nothing that we would be known
Few person who remember us have flown
Our work place is etching to get rid of us
Progeny sweating to take over our habitat.
We were mover and shaker of yesterday
We are but mute spectators of the day.
We are heroes and villains of our life
Lost in vanity, pain and arrogant strife.

## 38. GOOD DAYS SHALL BE HERE AGAIN.

Regular routine of nature amaze me
Even comets have exact periodicity
How they defy all forces known to man
Come and go as if they have no bondage.

Only bound state are birth and death
Man may rise as per deed and creed
Some defy death at every step and stage
Some infatuated with life are scared stiff

You shall not grieve when I am no more
I have defied life by being living dead
But destiny is not in anyone's control
Yet trusting in almighty tried my best.

You have right to gloat over my failures
But there is some success in every failure
I still believe and I do fondly hope
Good days shall be here again.
Days remain same as they were
Your thinking makes the difference
Surrender your thought with the Self
find that good day are here again

*Comments attached*

# 39. I DO NOT REALLY KNOW

Waves are result of turbulent sea
We behold the waves and admire
Few have wisdom to fathom the sea
Pursuer of worldly glamour
Be lost in play of hypocrisy
Do feel the hard ground of reality

Wise men have visualized
Decaying effects with time
Liaison with glamour is transitory
Why pursue shadow, I am sorry.

Ever binding into bondage
Of pain and heedlessness
How can you be really happy
But happiness is also a bondage
If not transformed into bliss
How – well I don't really know.

*Comments attached*

## 40. LIFE STILL CONTINUES ANYWAY

Lived frugally for fifty five summers
Seems I have developed a habit of it
Minimum wants and maximum profit.
Profit does not thrill me anymore.

Valued Discipline and punctuality
Remaining sincere and hardworking
Looking for more pay and promotion.
Promotion I don't strive anymore.

Strained myself physically and mentally
Keeping my performance next to none
More degrees and positions ensued.
Performance I am not crazy anymore.

Some time ago I loved fun and frolic
Beauties and brains were my mates
I was loved and regarded by all.
Fun I don't dream of it anymore.

I loved and respected my family
Spending quality time I could afford
Facing separation I pined helplessly.
Family does not bond me anymore.

Festivals would enthuse fresh action
Many a fountain of fire have I negotiated
In my effort to gather benign attention.
Festivals don't fetch reaction anymore.

Friends of school ware lost in college
College friends were lost in university
Transferable job scattered friendship.
Friendship does not entice anymore

Time lingeringly demand introspection
Why am I like this and not like that
I have no role model or benchmark
Introspection does trouble me anyway.

I am restlessly searching for rest
But craving for unbounded adventure
Led to accelerated degradation of life
Life still kicks and continue anyway.
success in external world is at the cost of inner domain
I shall now cleanse soiled inner entity for Your acceptance

# 41. HOW TO LIVE BEYOND MODES OF NATURE

Human being has choice to achieve peace though has time, money and energy constrain. Some points suggested for implementation to achieve peace while living.

Physical domain

1. Do not seek explanation or provide explanation. It does not change attitude of interrogator or responder.
2. Shun company of persons who weigh everything by money. Without human values money does not bring peace.
3. Keep your body fit and mind alert to enjoy peace.
4. Inculcate discipline. It helps you in enjoying the routine
5. Your sensitivities must not surface or else friends and foe shall take advantage and disturb your peace.
6. Women and wealth is indicator prosperity, but indulgence in them shall disturb your peace.
7. Before you comment relax.
8. Avoid name dropping and bragging. It belittles you.
9. Keep some time to yourself. Physical exercise and meditation recharges you.
10. Don't loose character to win reputation. Reputation is transitory and disturb peace

Mental domain

1. Violence begets violence only. It is an enemy of peace.
2. Watch and be aware calmly of your surrounding. Your calm disposition shall infuse calmness in others
3. Success is shifting sand, do not be overjoyed and You should not brood over failure. It is brooding that disturbs peace.
4. Control anger and depression.Do not allow it to linger. You shall only burn your own blood and loose peace
5. With positive attitude ensure co operation. You are as strong as your hands and legs. You gain nothing by confrontation
6. do not waste energy on negative things-arrogance and heedlessness

Spiritual Domain

1. Do not seek cause – the world is causeless, Cause and effect are valid in physical domain only, There are hidden layers in mental and spiritual domain that defy cause and effect.
2. Your peace should depend on you only. Attraction and repulsion is rooted in all sense objects. They disturb peace
3. Do not claim any work as your own, let others credit it to you.

Before long you shall find you are unaffected by modes of nature and in peace.

## 42. LIVING FREE

I was always prepared to die gracefully
It is living honorably that bothers me
Living has inexhaustible wants
Living has many essential duties
Living has to meet social requirements
Living has to live up to others expectation.
Living restlessly is searching for rest
Living constantly striving for promotion
Living you compromise in all your yearnings
Living is bent upon standards improving.
Lord also has his own scheme of things
Does not recognize you till you are for living.
 'you have lived life Fairly and fearlessly,
you were always free, 'choice was yours'
all the struggling and suffering was in vain
Now you tell me I was always free
'All the struggling and suffering you chose'
'Yes it is true, I did not consult you then.'

## 43. TWO TREES BY THE RIVER

Two trees by the river side
Gave it rare beauty and pride
Trees joined to form a canopy
With Fun and frolic were happy
Time passed green cover decreased
Summer losses were partially replaced
Fun and frolic ebbed and then ceased
The two trees were really scared.
One tree was denuded facing the sun
other one submerged itself in the river.
Both met their end as nature's game
Dried up tree was cut and burned
Softened by water other tree rotted.
One gave warmth other dirty stink

Today two trees do not exist by the river
Warmth of one and stink of other linger.
Human nurtured by river of lust, greed and anger
Choice is yours, so please do ponder and wonder
To remain dipped in the river and leave stink behind
Or to shun the river and leave warmth all around.

# SOME COMMENTS AND THEIR RESPONSES

## BOOK III.
## ATTRIBUTES AND FUNCTIONALITIES OF LIFE

### 24. SO WHAT IF I AM A BUBBLE

**Sujit Lala**
*Nicely expressed :-the inner truth! Thanks for sharing!*

**Somnath Banerjee in reply to Sujit Lala**
*Welcome sujit,*
*did not know that you were interested in spirituality.*
*thanks for your comment*

**Somnath Banerjee**
*Truth by definition is attributeless*

**Shekhar Ray**
*Nice & Thoughtful. I appreciate the message imbibed in it.*

**Somnath Banerjee in reply to Shekhar Ray**
*We differ a shade from birds of passage*
*we come with a mission and leave a message.*

**Sreeram Manoj Kumar**
*E X C E L L E N T. ................. Thank you for sharing Somnath ji*
*:):):):):):):):)*

**Somnath Banerjee in reply to Sreeram Manoj Kuma...**
*Thanks.the article is not as per scripture, with you profound knowledge bring out the differences*

**Sreeram Manoj Kumar in reply to Somnath Banerjee**
*Difference????? come on Somnath ji you are embarrassing the scriptures...... Who knows that the author of this poem does not have the essence of scriptures in his sub-conscious mind which might have sparkled out into conscious???????*

**Somnath Banerjee in reply to Sreeram Manoj Kuma...**
*I am the auther and you are right I know the essence, I do not quote the scripture like to bring out latest findings of science*

# 30. LIFE IS INTOXICANT

**Sudhakar Panda**
*Intoxicating analysis*

**Somnath Banerjee in reply to Sudhakar Panda**
*Any hangover*

**Divyanshu Tiwari**
*Highly thought provoking.an appreciable one!!!!*

**Somnath Banerjee in reply to Divyanshu Tiwari**
*Are you in craze for something, no negative thought shall near you.*

**Swatantra Sharma**
*That's like being a yogi in bliss.*

**Somnath Banerjee in reply to Swatantra Sharma**
*You may not be a yogi, any craze shall break all the barrier and reach bliss beautiful deduction, yogi generally intoxicated in spiritual bliss.*

**Ranganathan Ganapathy**
*Variety is the spice of life, need to enjoy the vibrancy of life.*

**Somnath Banerjee in reply to Ranganathan Ganapa...**
*Vibrancy of life in the intoxicant that you enjoy.*
*You have to choose from the variety presented be crazy about it it will lead to bliss swami Vivekananda said 'if you concentrate your soul force on one thing, there is nothing in the three world that you cannot get;*

**Shekhar Ray**
*Good one. ....... thought provoking.*

**Somnath Banerjee in reply to Shekhar Ray**
*I hope thought provoked were pleasent*

**Sunita Gupta**
*Nice post ----spirituality helps self to get out of mental turmoil like that !*

**Somnath Banerjee in reply to Sunita Gupta**
*When you enjoy pain and pleasure of physical and mental domain, mind is calm.*
*you have reached spiritual domain and all turmoil ceases.*

**Sunita Gupta in reply to Somnath Banerjee**
*Well, you need to keep counselling self on regular basis --till it becomes a habit for the mind to think in order !*

**Somnath Banerjee in reply to Sunita Gupta**
*Very true! once mind is calm no bubble burst- no turmoil*

**Sunita Gupta in reply to Somnath Banerjee**
*Thanks and regards Sir !*

**Somnath Banerjee in reply to Sunita Gupta**
*Happily enjoy life*

**Sunita Gupta in reply to Somnath Banerjee**
*Regards !*

**Rituparna Roy Chowdhury**
*User blocked by admin*

**Somnath Banerjee in reply to Rituparna Roy Chow...**
*There are no constraints on the human mind, no walls around the human spirit, no barriers to our progress except those we ourselves erect. when life is intoxicant you are into volition. Progress is assured. please remember we all are progressing from manifest to unmanifest*

## 32. REALITIES OF LIFE

**Saroj Das**
*Life and Mind are not the same;*
*Life is God, Mind is the man.*

*At present, Life is experiencing Life through a Mind.*
*Goal:- Life must experience Life without the help of a mind.*
*\*Mind can not experience anything without Life.., therefore.*

**Somnath Banerjee in reply to Saroj Das**
*Where does consciousness fits in.*
*life element is reflection of god or subtle element as defined in gita.*
*Excellent inferences, regards*

**Saroj Das in reply to Somnath Banerjee**
*Matter has some properties. Therefore, it can be defined. Since Consciousness has no properties, it, therefore, can not be related to anything. Everything happens IN life; nothing happens TO life.*

*According to the Geeta, Creator God (total mind) has been defined as beyond the eight states of nature (matter) in the verse 5th of chapter 7. Regards.*
*sd//*

### Somnath Banerjee in reply to Saroj Das
*The eight state of nature are five basic element of physical domain earth, water, fire, air and ether and three mental domain mind, intellect and ego and in spiritual domain the life element*

*This life element ( spiritual domain)upholds the universe ( physical Domain). is this life element like a catalyst whose interaction with 8 states of nature give rise to consciousness*

### Saroj Das in reply to Somnath Banerjee
*"This life element like a catalyst whose interaction with 8 states of nature give rise to consciousness"...*

*The waking state ego (Conscious) and the dream state ego (subconscious), both are conditioned by Cause and Effect.....(in time and space).*

*The sleeping state (Unconscious) ego is conditioned by the CAUSE only.*

*LIFE (Awareness) is a witness to all the above three states of consciousness.*

*Let me try to make it simple..*

*I (ego) am Aware of my waking state consciousness, I was aware of my subconscious while i was dreaming..., and i am Aware of their absence (conscious and subconscious) while i was asleep.*

*This Awareness is not an element.*

### Somnath Banerjee in reply to Saroj Das
*Thank you for your critical analysis.*

*Today the integrated information can quantify the consciousness which is aggregation of brain activity.. it can correctly predict the three states of consciousness.*

*I agree with you that life is an operator and not an element. its operation results in consciousness and awareness*

**Saroj Das**

*1 Man and universe mismatch.................A. Universe is an extention of the mind.*

*2.life divided in two parts............................Life has no parts.*

*a. pre death period - life in the world.......Death is the other name of the term, 'Change'.*

*b. post death period – life in paradise....The birth of youth is the post death period of childhood. (Paradise)!!*

**Somnath Banerjee in reply to Saroj Das**
*Very good observation.*

**Mrxexon**

*I can only say that the spirit inside of each person is the same.*

*When coming to this earth, we begin to hang things on ourselves according to what we believe ourselves to be. This gives us our individuality. In returning to God, we backtrack through where we once walked, and we discard the things we once thought important.*

*When we arrive home, we are as empty and naked as the day we were born. And this is in spite of what religion one embraces in life. It is the natural way of things, as all things return to their source sooner or later.*

*One can go crazy from trying to follow all the rules some religions have. Just be a kind and compassionate person, and watch the right path magically appear beneath your feet.*

**Somnath Banerjee in reply to Mrxexon**
*Without prejudice to any religion do evaluate metaphysically the realities enunciated.regarding your comment1spirit is same- why this assumption.. coming down --hanging things... do you think it possible.*

*As all things return to their source sooner or later.- is it like battery.. current starting from + and returning to -ve lastly do not go crazy- millions of intelligent people believe in them.. every founder of religion say they came from GOD*

**Abc Narayan**
*Religion is like a study course for learning knowledge and enriching our intellectuality. It is more connected for our learning*

*and understanding knowledge, and much less connected with our journey of life. Many people, both before as well as after graduating a course of study, consider the course itself is great and highest peak of everything. And, this is happening due to their ego, because they are simply forgetting that this course is only a means to enrich their basic knowledge and intellectuality in order to help them perform in their further study and work in the path of social and spiritusl living. The real and true religion is a guidance which teaches people to understand true way of living with good social attitude and with high spirituality.*

### *Somnath Banerjee in reply to Abc Narayan*
*'The real and true religion is a guidance which teaches people to understand true way of living with good social attitude and with high spirituality.' you are absolutely correct.highlighted realities have been accepted by more than billion people. do they reflect*

*1 guidance*
*2 understand true way of living*
*3 good social attitude*
*4 spirituality.*

### *Abc Narayan in reply to Somnath Banerjee*
*Nice and true observation.*

### *Somnath Banerjee in reply to Abc Narayan*
*Your views on realities is invited*

## 34. ONLY TWO THINGS OF LIFE

### *Raju Adhunuri*
*Rightly said ji what ever the thing which is going to our life be consciousness*

### *Somnath Banerjee in reply to Raju Adhunuri*
*Consciousness is the expectation value of life operator operating on the energy centres of the brain.*

### *Pavan Raina*
*Right Somenath jee. Consciousness is free data in space and for connectivity with the right data at the right time the highest level of integrity only has the capability in this civilized world. Regards.*

**Somnath Banerjee in reply to Pavan Raina**
*Pawanji,*
*consciousness is born out of interaction of life with energy centers*
*of the brain. it is part of mind.interaction of the consciousness takes*
*place out side the body with help of senses. data in space are sense*
*objects which are accessed by senses processed by our mind into*
*information.*

**Pavan Raina in reply to Somnath Banerjee**
*Thanks for the clarification.*

**Somnath Banerjee in reply to Pavan Raina**
*Welcome*

## 36. Detachment from the world

**Sanghamitra Konwar**
*Nice thought on self realization. .*

**Somnath Banerjee in reply to Sanghamitra Konwar**
*YOU PLAY WITH YOURSELF BE LOST IN YOURSELF*
*YOU ARE YOUR WORLD BY YOURSELF*
*YOU ARE god OF YOUR WORLD.*

**Sanghamitra Konwar in reply to Somnath Banerjee**
*Well said..*

**Somnath Banerjee in reply to Sanghamitra Konwar**
*Thanks*

**Surendra Pal**
*How true! We go through life grabbing one thing after another and*
*become depressed if we lose them. Real happiness can come only if*
*we maintain inner peace regardless of what happens.*

**Somnath Banerjee in reply to Surendra Pal**
*Easier said than done as detachment from world leads attachment*
*with ego. Inner peace comes when you subdue ego.*

**Raju Paighan**
*Great suggestion !!!*
*Thanks*

*Madhusudan Attaluri in reply to Raju Paighan*

*Somnath Banerjee in reply to Madhusudan Attalur...*
*Read it again, detachment--attachment--realization and joy*

*Madhusudan Attaluri in reply to Somnath Banerjee*
*I expect you to put it in your own words. If not willing, it is O.K.
Gratitude.*

*Somnath Banerjee in reply to Madhusudan Attalur...*
*You should not fight Life/*

## 38. Good days shall be here again.

*Sajal Gupta*
*Nice post*

*Somnath Banerjee in reply to Sajal Gupta*
*Thanks*

*Koshi Munshi*
*Lovely share. I am attracted to the title in particular, it says everything
so clearly. Just like day follows night, joy follows sorrow, good days
are bound to come soon...whatever is new becomes old, after that a
transformation has to happen for goodness to be restored...*

*Somnath Banerjee in reply to Koshi Munshi*
*Transition from physical to mental to spiritual domain with ambient
condition remaining same bliss follows*

*Koshi Munshi in reply to Somnath Banerjee*
*Well expressed Sir..Thank u..*

*Somnath Banerjee in reply to Koshi Munshi*
*Welcome*

*Koshi Munshi in reply to Somnath Banerjee*
*Well expressed Sir..Thank u..*

*Somnath Banerjee in reply to Koshi Munshi*
*WELCOME*

*Ajeet Singh*
*Nice...........*

*Somnath Banerjee in reply to Ajeet Singh*
*Increasing my confidence*

## 39 How I do not really know

*Dp Sharma*
*We should break all bondage for merger with infinity.*

*Somnath Banerjee in reply to Dp Sharma*
*Sorry you cannot break all bondages*

*Dp Sharma in reply to Somnath Banerjee*
*You are right that I cannot break all bondage but my perception and conviction is that ONE can.*

*Somnath Banerjee in reply to Dp Sharma*
*Life operates on life bondages new life*
*When under stress strives to be free*
*Free before birth,*
*Free after death*

*Food for your visualization and stabilization*

# BOOK IV
# FUNCTIONAL MIND

# BOOK IV FUNCTIONAL MIND

# 44. MIND EVOLVES

When I drink and loose myself
 In the stupor of maddening mirth
The world around me is rosy
As ejaculation of spirit commences
...............and mind ceases
Trying to solve a technical problem
The day is lost in trance
Night redefines the problem
Solution now is very near
..................And mind hangs
When I indulge in yogic slumber
Mind is numb and nerves calm
 As I enjoy the unfolding peace
Captivating the heightened awareness
...............and mind evaporates
My otherwise alert and agile mind
Has crashed unintended many a time
As my life function seeks new horizon
And I find it palpating in higher domain
....................And mind realizes.
Operation of life function modifies the mind
Mind does not stop at 'nothingness'
It now functions in attribute of soul
Enjoying the play of modes of nature
...............And mind evolves.

*Comments attached*

## 45. HOW CAN I BE CALM

Wise men have advised to make mind calm
I asked my mind 'why are you agitated'
'Billion neurons are sending electric shocks
With sensing from the external world
And contribution from brain complexes of inner world
How can I be calm,
Now see how I do functions for you.'
I have with me intellect and your virtual image Ego,
Data in the neural fabric is processed into information
It is for intellect to decide on the action to be taken
Ego either vetoes it or I send the decision for action,
All these I do in a fraction of second and am ready for next.'
So how can I be calm even you may want me to be.

## 46. CALMMING THE MIND

I closed all the senses shutting the external world
By meditating, with consciousness at tip of nose
'Now dear mind can you be calm', 'partially;
Said mind 'thinking process does not abate'
Then I tried transcendental meditation
I left my mind alone sitting calmly
Soon I reached so called alpha state
My mind was calm for a short period.
Faced with a problem, Mind would think
Out the situation, Courses of action,
Suggest solution and help in implementation
But now mind does not think anymore.
Now I can only listen, cannot react.
Sense of doer ship has lost meaning
All my knowledge looks outdate
My life also refuses further guidance
Can you help me reboot my mind?

# 47. SANDWICHED BETWEEN LIFE AND MIND

Life gives conscience and mind gives consciousness. After pursuing Phd in Nuclear Engineering for four years, I was selected to be an army officer. my conscience said dont go, my father said dont go but mind said go- a chance in life time, life wanted status quo but mind reminded 'life is for change'.

All brain complexes got active each exercising his priority, with so many vibrational modes of the mento-emotional energy (thoughts)

My intellect was jammed. My life had been my loving mate, it always agreed with me. in this case also it did not argue or disagree but posed some questions for deliberation

1. You are physically unfit.
   Mind replied : training will make me fit
2. Army life is different
   Mind said : fear of unknown is foolish, 10 lakh people are in the army.
3. You will not have domestic life
   Mind said we shall cross the bridge when we come to it.
4. You shall loose all your friends both male and female
   Mind pondered over the statement and finally said 'Lord Krishna also left all his friends and weNt to Mathura.
5. You shall take oath to serve at the peril of your life.
   Mind. That is what makes it glorious. What better way is there to die facing odd for the motherland.

Heroics of 1971 was still fresh in my mind.

Life of a technical graduate in the academy is miserable to say the least. My transformation from human life to an efficient machine serving beyind the call of duty. There is no love or compassion. Only Duty. This superficial army life boosted my ego by false sense of honor and dignity.After few years of partying and drinking I asked mt mind 'are you happy of your achievements' Mind kept quiet for sometime and said 'I am hungry not for food but for knowledge'

See how my domains are starving. 'I possibly cannot change my job now, there is twenty years of bond.' Well find solution within constrain.

*Comments attached*

# 48. DEFENSE OF EGO

When a cat sees himself in mirror a lion There is aberration in its perception Or mirror is tricky, mischievous one Or ambient condition lead to wrong conclusion. A man creates image of himself in the mind It has all the attributes and function defining him The operating system of life is defined. Benchmark to external stimulus highlighted. Decision of your intellect – logical and emotional is Vetoed. This is ego, supreme commander of Physical and mental domain.

Some compare it to mighty demon. Your material success depends upon it It is the source of will power It has great motivational value. Your propensities both real and imaginary are refined by it. You can never neutralize it You can boost or deplete some of its Application when your survival depends upon it. Ego and knowledge are inversely proportional. As Einstein states. "True when knowledge increases ego minimizes." In thought process the mind can be looked upon as data forwarding plane inter facing The organ of senses and organ of action.

For decision making it is dependent on intellect (both logic and emotion representing head and heart The thought is parallel processed by intellect, ego and soul. Soul only advices but ego can veto. More Knowledge, more sharp intellect less veto is required Human system then gain maturity. There is another source of input to ego. It interfaces with Soul. It is that part of the brain that generates voice of Conscience- suggests to you what is right and what is wrong. Two cases can arise one, Ego Vetoes soul and the other Ego agrees with the soul. When ego gets minimized the input from attributes of the soul gets boosted and transmitted directly to the mind. The Man is Spiritual

*Comments attached*

# 49. EGO & ENLIGHTENMENT

Sai Baba propounded two cardinal principle of attitude and perseverance for realization of self and for success in life. Both involve control of mind" There are two ways of controlling the mind. "Either sever its connection with all things, or establish a connection of it with everything "said sage Vasishtha.

Acharya Sankara was in the Kutir, and the door was bolted from within. One of the disciples came and knocked. "Who is that?" asked the Master.
"I" was the answer.
"Oh I ! Either reduce it to zero or expand it to infinity !" retorted the Master from within.
Please do note I or Ego or mind involve each other. It can be three type
"I am this body."
"I am nothing. "
"I am everything."
There is no harm if we feel that we are nothing. "I" is non doer. Leads to equamity

There is also no harm if we feel that we are everything. "I" is god of his world also leads to equamity

But if we feel that we are only something, then we are caught.

I am physically fit and mentally alert and this I is like a tree, if it is very small the goats shall gobble it up,and if it is very tall, it will be broken in the storm. This is dilemma of being something.

*Some job interview questions that are guaranteed to come up regardless of your industry, your experience level, and job type universal and much-dreaded classic: "Tell me about yourself."*

Mind you he has your biodata in front of him. You start with "I am .....name, family background, education experience hobbies and what have you. But you have forgotten to justify your suitability for the job in question

*You might have lost the opportunity provided.*

*Have you noticed*
1. *Your I is adaptable*
2. *It is programmable*
3. *Inherited qualities can be masked*
4. *Your I changes with the role.*
5. *You loose doer ship as you age.*
6. *Your knowledge gets obsolete*
7. *Your pious life leads to vanity*
8. *Without I, you don't exist.*
9. *Your pain pleasure and struggle end with end of I.*
10. *When mind surrenders to life you are enlightened.*

## 50. MAKING YOU FEARLESS

The training drill for a section of troops under fire is

DASH, DOWN, CRAWL, OBSERVE, SIGHTS, & FIRE.

During training exercises they made us repeat it again and again till it became our second nature. One day I enquired its logic from our platoon commander, he said magnanimously ' the bullet you hear has not taken your life as speed of bullet is higher than the speed of sound', "Sir after Dashing to cover why go Down". "Figure it out yourself damn it". So I pondered.

A bullet from rifle tends to rise approximately six feet in 500 yards so going down, you escape the enemy. You change your position by crawling out of view of the enemy. From the concealed position you observe ready for counter attack, sight the enemy and fire.

You have become fearless with confidence in yourself, on your weapon and training.

"In wealth is the fear of poverty, in knowledge the fear of ignorance, in beauty the fear of age, in fame the fear of backbiters, in success the fear of jealousy, even in body is the fear of death. Everything in this earth is fraught with fear. He alone is fearless who has given up everything" (Vairâgya-Shatakam, 31) like a soldier on the battle field.

Life is full of accidents, coincidence, and incidents where you face trauma, disability and catastrophe. You have survived means that the occurrence has not been fatal. You apply the above drill mentally and you shall be able to live life fearlessly. Being numb, not able to react is detrimental to your welfare. Lie low, regroup yourself, seek opportunity and with renewed vigor fight back. mind must choose fight and not flight.

Your love for life is mitigated under separation from first love, financial loss due to speculative venture, immoral or illegal action due to anger, disease and disaster. You are not dead but your fighting spirit is depleted. life now crawls, never mind, set your revised target overcoming your disability and depression.

Aim is to show that mind is programmable, fear exists only in mind. Fearlessness IS independent of you propensities- goodness, passion or delusion.

*Comments attached*

# 51. LORD IN CONSCIENCE

If you establish lord in your conscience then your voice of conscience shall be Lords voice. You are in communion with lord all the time or whenever you require. You have no power to veto the Voice. There is no duality problem any more. The thinking process gets minimized Your mind and intellect are in communication with lord. Ego finds solace in surrendering to lords will. You exist as an entity devoted to welfare and development of human life

Are you enlightened? you may not be. Are you above modes of nature? you may not be.Are you above lust, greed and anger? You may or may not be.Shall you develop compassion? You may or may not. Will you be immune to diseases? You may not. Are your senses in your control? They may or may not be in full control. Will you be healthy physically? You may not be. Will you have vanity of saints? You may or may not. Will you feel pain from your passion? Yes you shall. Will your drinking give you hangover? Yes if not in moderation. Will you have choice of doing things in your own way? No, you will be constrained. Will attachment persist? It shall not be apparent.

'What do you mean by surrendering to Lord?'. You listen to whatever lord says. You accept him as your controller and as a controller of everything. You don't rebel. You follow his instructions precisely, You depend upon him for results. You do your job but depend up on him for protection. You accept the fact that you are not controllers but only Lord is the controller. You become his servants. You follow his orders. Once you do this, you become karma-free and go back to his place, where there is no misery and is eternal. Similar reasoning applies to our desires, ambitions, thoughts, ideas etc.

'Are you not free to act? Are you simply supposed to act like slave to Lord'. You are creating a lot of karma here if you act on your own ways. Once you follow Lord's instructions, you become karma free. Which is better? To follow your own ideas and become bound by karmic reactions; or follow and surrender to Lord and become karma free? You need to decide that for yourself. Does that mean you loose your personality? NO. you will follow Lord's instructions which will eventually bring the best in you and will make your life more enjoyable and blissful. Lord says, "Do as you wish!". You experiment yourself and decide for yourself. My Lord Krishna is like my loving mate who agrees with me in all decision, I only know it is all his decision that I abide.

# 52. MY MIND DOES NOT THINK ANYMORE

All these three score years I was proud
Of my mind -alert, agile, a thinking hub
Many honors and degrees bear testimony
Now my mind does not think any more.
'I would like a few word with you, dear mind'
Sluggishly mind replied' yes, what is it this time'
I told you to think about job prospects
Mind said 'you have retired from Job'
Well what about the land project
Many inputs are missing so no thinking
All my question it answered readily
And then mind relaxed immediately
CAN YOU HELP ME TO MAKE MY MIND THINK.?

*Comments attached*

# 53. WHAT IS YOUR WORLD?

Your mind has attributes and functionalities of logic and emotions spatially distributed in your brain.

This your world. External world may paint many pictures ( interaction of senses with sense objects), but only those which are accepted by mind get into your world. physically it means that out of 5 billion human populating earth only those people form your world who share your pains and pleasure and you share theirs. You shall find not more than 20-25 persons are part of your world and couple ofthem in work place.

Some advantages are clear
Compassion: both Love and war persists yet compassion is guaranteed..

- God is responsible. you are god of your world, you are responsible for your livelihood.
- Change is only constant in your world
- Knowledge Every experience shall yield knowledge.. sense object- senses-mind- intellect- ego- knowledge.
- Equamity is not easy as Arjun pointed out.
- Every where is GOD In your world it is your attributes and functionalities.
- Happiness. State of bliss unaffected by ambient condition is real happiness
- Introvert is full of happiness. Love and cough cannot be hidden so is happiness
- Silence You can bring about peace by silence.
- Be aware of Fame, Lust and money In your world you are not deluded by these

# 54. WHAT YOU GO FOR, YOU HAVE TO FORGO

What you go for, you have to forgo
What you say, many have said before
Causes of life, you find it causeless
Be happy, spread happiness all the way

What made you happy yesterday
Does not makes you happy today.
Spread your ' I' gracefully and carefully
its intensive and extensive expansion has no limit.

A man is born that is he gains consciousness
With associated inherent characteristics
A fusion of genes interaction with mutation
He is small and his world is also small.

Interaction of consciousness begins
He identifies and learns continuously
He establishes an image in his mind
This is your "I" with its inherent values.

You go for physical and social development
After back breaking effort, win women and gold
Your life cycle revolve around career Development
Family. Friends, fun and festival involvement

Years roll by, you are God of your world
All your time is lost in meeting trade offs
physical strength is decreasing function of time
Social involvement reduces to spectator mode.

You have lived your life in physical and mental domain
Your 'I' had expanded and then shrunk in vain
your world also expanded, on superannuation shrunk
what do you do now, what can you do now.

Your mind has to surrender to life functionalities
Your bloated ego has to reconcile with conscience
A domain change to spiritual is necessaty
You have to forgo both women and gold.
With love and compassion your world expands
Your reduced ego then encompasses all.

# COMMENTS AND RESPONSES BY SEEKERS AMD MASTERS OF SPEAKING TREE TOI

## BOOK IV. FUNCTIONAL MIND

### 44. MIND EVOLVES

**Susil Kumar Bandopadhyay**
*"Enjoying the play of mind mature and evolves". Thanks for sharing this nice blog "Mind Evolves".*

**Somnath Banerjee in reply to Susil Kumar Bandop...**
*Thanks, may your mind evolve to new horizon*

**Applique Oitet**
*Beautiful presentation :-) :-) :-) :-)*

**Somnath Banerjee in reply to Applique Oitet**
*Thanks and gratitude, reached higher state, Lord bless you*

**Shekhar Ray**
*Nice thoughts. ... especially the last one. .. very true. .... Mind does not stop at 'nothingness'........*

**Somnath Banerjee in reply to Shekhar Ray**
*Very true,may you be blessed with happiness*

### 47. Sandwiched between life and mind

**Sumeet Agrawal**
*Need to balance*

**Somnath Banerjee in reply to Sumeet Agrawal**
*What can you balence life or mind.
think & tell me*

**Venkataramanaiah Ramu**
*Dear Somnath, it appears that U have not landed in a correct spot. Army may not be a correct placement for people like U who probably may be having in mind to use ur knowledge or further*

*enhance the same etc., whereas army is 90% discipline, and the balance option for u to decide. U may have to keep ur enthu aside till u are a part of that stream and by the time U are out, it is possible that ur stream may also be quite different in tune with ur 20 years of service in the army, U also may become a disciplinarian and like to see more discipline around u and less of other things.*

**Somnath Banerjee in reply to Venkataramanaiah R...**
*Mind is turbulent, choice that man has is also limited lastly whatever happens always happens and man has to sdapt to it.*
*yet no knowledge is wasted. knowledge and action leads to devotion*

## 48. DEFENSE OF EGO

**Kalavathi Sonti**
*More knowledge less ego,by,Einstien,!!!The less ego, more no ego there is only ONE!!!vedanha in a tablet.nice..*

**Somnath Banerjee in reply to Kalavathi Sonti**
*All instinctive action in humans are modified by EGO. Ego is not one but can be modified whereas soul is not within purview of humans to change*

**Sunita Gupta**
*Nicely presented ----defense of ego ?*

**Somnath Banerjee in reply to Sunita Gupta**
*Thanks but people do not appreciate ego.*

**Sunita Gupta in reply to Somnath Banerjee**
*Is your ego is sustaining you or it is demeaning others ----there lies the difference*

## 50. MAKING YOU FEARLESS

**Bipin Chandra**
*The Self is the Absolute. Because it is also inside us – it is our pure subjectivity – it is called the Self or the Atman. Because it is not merely inside us but everywhere, it is a universal plenum*

*of completion.A citizen is fully protected by the laws wherein and whereby he is a citizen. We are citizens of the universe, and the universe will protect us. We are guarded from all sides. We are never without a friend and we have no enemies, because the world has come round into a point of singular observation of a totality of Awareness. The power of powers who gives power to the mind and the support of supports on which the mind rests is Brahman or Atman (microcosmic level).... abiding on which all fears will vanish in toto...... thanks and regards sir.*

### Somnath Banerjee in reply to Bipin Chandra
*What you say is absolutely correct. so as Upanishads and Buddha said.the path suggested by you is long and time consuming.*

*What i have highlighted is very simple way to become fearless.Here both follower of God and Devil can become fearless*

### Pavan Raina
*This helps me to increase my spirits and try to see beyond mundane mind wandering of non essential worries.*

### Somnath Banerjee in reply to Pavan Raina
*Fearless your mind does not wander. you carryout your duties - observing the need and sighting the target.*

## 52. MY MIND DOES NOT THINK ANYMORE

### Pavan Raina
*Where is the requirement for MIND to think and add complications. The MIND which has been trying to act as king and creating torture has been imprisoned and has become a tool of intellect and in the present case the MIND has become a mere messenger. That is a wonderful state many young people have to understand. Nice thoughts sir.*

### Somnath Banerjee in reply to Pavan Raina
*Thank you for your kind words.*

### Bhuvenarendra Gupta
*Mind is like computer.You have to store correct inputs then only it will give you correct outputs.As they say garbage in*

*garbage out. When mind becomes old it starts getting viruses like computer. We should accept the fact with old age.*

**Somnath Banerjee in reply to Bhuvenarendra Gupt...**
*Mind is part of the computer human have, it is more like an operating system, mind of humans do not deteriorate at sixty. Not thinking state of mind you please investigate and come out with solution to help me.*

BOOK V

RANDOM RESULTS OF
HARMONISED LIFE AND MIND

# BOOK V
## RANDOM RESULTS OF HARMONISED
## LIFE AND MIND

## COMMENTS

## 55. A POOR MAN LIKE ME FULL OF FEAR

A poor man like me full of fear
Finds no time to seek or share.
I am an old man full of care
What can I do but coolly stare

Days gone by my strength was rare
An alert mind full of vim and vigor
Many a beauty I had won fair and square
 Many a degrees were awarded everywhere.

I was humored and honored in every sphere
With bright eyes and warm heart, my dear.
Only my loving mate did not change ever
He knows all my secrets, I know none

Fear disappear when He is there
 I have no need to seek or share
He is my delight in every sphere
I don't bullshit in feigned anger.

Affinity for woman looks ridiculous
Craze for wealth looks credulous
My mate is their true owner
 I am his unworthy custodian.

He cannot be seen by any one
Only guides me in every occasion
I do as per his beguine direction
I am joyful in every location.

His abode is my conscience, my dear
I have installed Lord Krishna in there.

*Comments attached*

159

# 56. BEAUTY AND UGLY BOTH HAVE EQUAL WORKMANSHIP

Beauty

Beauty is a characteristic of a person, animal, place, object or idea that provides a perpetual experience of pleasure and satisfaction. An "ideal beauty" is an entity which is admired, or possesses features widely attributed to beauty in a particular culture, for perfection. There is evidence that perceptions of beauty are evolutionarily determined, that things, aspects of people and landscapes considered beautiful are typically found in situations likely to give enhanced survival of the perceiving human's genes.

Ugly

Ugliness is a property of a person or thing that is unpleasant to look upon and results in a highly unfavorable evaluation. To be ugly is to be aesthetically unattractive, repulsive, or offensive. People who appear ugly to others suffer well-documented discrimination, earning 10 to 15 percent less per year than similar workers, and are less likely to be hired for almost any job, but lack legal recourse to fight discrimination.

Abraham Lincoln

For some people, ugliness is a central aspect of their persona. Famous in his own time for his perceived ugliness, Abraham Lincoln was described by a contemporary: "to say that he is ugly is nothing; to add that his figure is grotesque, is to convey no adequate impression." However, his looks proved to be an asset in his personal and political relationships, as his law partner William Herndon wrote, "He was not a pretty man by any means, nor was he an ugly one; he was a homely man, careless of his looks, plain-looking and plain-acting. He had no pomp, display, or dignity, so-called. He appeared simple in his carriage and bearing. He was a sad-looking man; his melancholy dripped from him as he walked. His apparent gloom impressed his friends, and created sympathy for him—one means of his great success."

Beholders eyes

what's beautiful to one person might actually be considered ugly to the next. After all, beauty is in the eye of the beholder. I am a masterpiece. I am a work of art. I have been made by the Master. I am a 'piece' of the Master, "For we are God's own handiwork (His beautiful workmanship). We are His design, His creation, His masterpiece…" (Ephesians 2:10) Beauty and Ugly both have equal workmanship.

## 57. BETTER HUMAN BEING

Like severely wounded tiger crawls back to the cave
Licking his wound with shattered pride
Fortnight after spinal surgery I came back home
Fully incapacited at everybody's mercy.

Gone were the arrogance of army colonel
Gone were the pride of university professor
Gone were the flexibility of yoga master
Gone were the skills of network architecture.

Friend looking at my pitiable state commented
' this is the result of lifelong Sin committed;
Though many retorts sprang in the mind
Eyes were moist and lips were closed.

lust evaporated in shattered physical state
Greed disappeared in fight for survival
Anger had to find in the roots of equamity
Only loving mate coaxed in path of recovery.

Days passed into weeks and weeks into months
The nerves grew strong and muscles responded
University that held me in esteem, discontinued my service
The banks were threatening to foreclose my pension
Friends and relatives were shunning my company
Servants were removing anything they found useful.
I progressed from Sitting supported to Sitting un supported
When I Kneeled I would shake like Chinese doll
Next I stood with walker and with three legged sticked
Lastly stick was not required, I could walk free.

After some time I joined an engineering collage
Alighting from the car I met the same friend
'It is profound grace of Almighty you are working again'
'It was His grace when I had fallen ill" I responded.

He did not understand. Lord had removed lust, greed and anger
I had become a better human having understood full surrender.

*Comments attached*

## 58. BEYOND LONELINESS

Yesterday loneliness spoke with yearning,
She had many questions, some were
Why are you silent and all alone?
Are you a person of equamity?
Don't you have social obligation?
Are you punishing yourself?
Shall it change course of event?
I answered them all in the negative.

She inquired' then why are you here all alone.
Whom do you want to impress
Wife – relationship can only strain,
Daughter – course of event shall not change her life
Friends – they shall all disappear.
What would you do with extra money earned?
Buy land but for whom.
House- you already have.
 Source of income- you have pension.
What you want in life?
I work for a bit of honor and dignity.
Loneliness was fed up with me

Honor spoke to me beseechingly
What a state I had downgraded it
From colonel to private collage teacher
Couldn't I have done something better?

Dignity spoke with venom
Wanted to desert me permanently
At least my spiritual need shall be met
You honor and dignity can both leave.

Truth which I had clasped to my heart
Wanted to follow her friends
I stopped her immediately
She had no ground to complain

Truth was eloquent in her silence
Dignity returned being frustrated without truth
Honor returned pining for dignity
Loneliness was lost in my status
I and my loving mate (truth) are together
Loneliness has no place in this sphere.

## 59. BODY GLOW

How long shall you remain intoxicated
How long shall you be led by instinct only
How long shall you devote to physical form
It is high time you wake up from this slumber.
 No one can awaken you except yourself,
Relinquishing doer ship you awaken
Shall you traverse in leaky tub sleeping
Be beyond worry yet worry haunts you
 Cool water in leaky tub is caressing
You did nothing but continued sleeping
On reaching nose it is suffocating
Frenzy action yet you are sinking
 Body glow comes from glow within
No beauty parlour can bleach it in.

*Comments attached*

# 60. CAN YOU JUSTIFY DECEPTION AS RELIGION

Today
Deception is religion
corruption the means
Profit is the motive.
conscience who cares.

you be Hindu, Muslim or Christian,
all are in clutch of multifarious deception
social, cultural, religious and self deception
conscience has lost its position.

You shall be considered smart and intelligent
You shall be source of providing happiness
Many a awkward situation prevented
Only time will paint mask of deceiver.

Logic may win but emotion shall fail
When deception enters your frame
Compassion dead and honesty butchered
Sitting on pile of notes, you brag success.

Brokers and sycophants encircle you
Sucking out your basic life survivability
Being blackmailed day in and day out
As you loose slowly but surely credibility.

So votaries of deception can you justify deception as religion
Which promises instant gratification and material success?

*Comments attached*

# 61. DURGA – CONFUSION TERMINATOR

With great pomp and show Goddess Durga has arrived. New clothes are worn, fun and frolics are rampant, prayer to grant wealth, beauty and success fills up the air with beating of drums, cymbals and fragrant smoke. Festivities continue throughout day and night, the whole area is decked up with shops of multiple hue, & cultural activities reach its peak.

It was so till one Durga Puja I asked my mother "what does Durga Puja Mean?".

She was quite for sometime and then said "you want to know, why?"

"well, I feel there is something more than what I know".

'Essence of this worship is that man must acquire multiple competency, then utilize animal aspects and kill his demonical nature. He is then successful in life, all his confusion destroyed. See goddess wielding weapons (Competencies) in each of her ten hands, riding the tiger (animal aspect) killing the demon Mahisasura. She has been named Durga which means confusion terminator and Mahisasur is the great ego in man". Her answer just clean bowled me.

After digesting the answer I again inquired "Do all men have Demonical nature?"

' yes, every person has saintly, demonical and beastly characteristic". 'Mummy, why should demon be killed, they look strong and powerful ?'

'Demons undertake hard work and sacrifice gaining multiple competencies and quickly dominate the Devas (saintly attributes) but they believe in sensual pleasure, greed and anger. They are hypocrite and arrogant. They have no peace – today I have gained this, tomorrow I shall gain that. This is mine today tomorrow that will also be mine. I am rich, powerful and famous. I shall enjoy I shall give alms. They do not believe in God. Their life becomes a continuous process of want, pain and misery. Do you want to be like that?'. ""Mummy, I now understand what you say then why include other four God and Goddesses."

Mother thought for a minute and said ' Goddess Durga was going for the battle so she required them'

'Mummy you said this battle is not real war, it is war in the mind' ;

'yes, these gods represent forces that help a person in his fight with demonical forces. You must have sufficient knowledge ( Saraswati), be well provided (Laxmi), have a protector (Kartika) and logistic controller (Ganesh). Without blessing from them you cannot fight. Now go and play '

One point lingered in my mind : if durga puja was for personality development then why so much pomp and show? It looked more for social interaction than religious overtures. Again finding mother in reflective mood I posed my question.

"All are forms of worship (Puja). Worship for self development, one sits in solitude concentrating on Self and realizing Self. All people cannot perform such worship they believe in Pomp and show, they gain wealth and fame for their effort and that is their aim. Goddess grants them beauty, wealth and fame. Lastly persons who drink alcohol or other intoxicant indulging in song and dance is also worshipping the same goddess for spiritual drunkenness which does not wane with time. Every person has his own way to worship".

I then listened to Chandi Path and was amazed by the birth of Goddess Durga, synthesis of energy leading to female form in the days when neither formation of stars from nebula was known nor was teleportation discovered. I again approached mother and inquired 'why female form was synthesized and what is its significance in real life'.

'Mahisasura had boon from creator (Bramha) that no man or God would be able to defeat him. Hence female form was synthesized, full beautiful and well decorated to entice and eliminate the demon. Seeing her beauty and grandeur Demon immediately fell in love for her and offered to marry her. When the offer was rejected, his lust and anger overtook him he ordered his soldier to seize her by force and bring her to him. Once they were defeated, he attacked with all skill and magical power. Battle raged on and ultimately she destroyed him. In real life it means that man cannot overcome Ego

( Greed, Lust and Anger) without help of woman, she first entice him with beauty and lust, then helps him in overcoming greed, lust and anger.'

'This is bit confusing, but how does Goddess Durga eliminate confusion'.

'To understand confusion you have understand how action originate. '

'yes, I know, some action require thinking and some are reflex'.

'All action require thinking, some action which are repetitive do not require rethinking, as their reactions are stored in the nerve centers. Most of action require thinking, in human being it is a complicated process. Based on the input from the sense organs, mind put forward details of previous action and reaction to the intellect(budhi). Intellect analyses the logical and emotional aspects, a train of thought is originated for decision to the ego (aham). Based on decision by Ego, communicated by intellect, mind sends command for the action. Confusion arises when more than one thought is generated by intellect and ego is not able decide on correct course of action or sometime two train of thought clash with one another, ego is unable to decide or ego does not like the action suggested. The soul is mere spectator or enjoyer. People devoted to Goddess have their ego to filter the action recommended through lust, greed and anger so that mind is clear and no confusion occur. The demonical thought shall arise in your mind as they guarantee instant gratification but with practice you shall be able to eliminate them.'

I loved the Devi mantra where existence of Goddess in all elements as mother, shadow, devotion, wealth, intelligence, energy etc.. and every time 'obeisance to you' is repeated 5 times. I got hold of mother just after her puja and posed my question. She gave me prasad and told me to disappear which I reluctantly did.

Durga puja ended and last day after sprinkling of water for peace was over I came home to pay obeisance to mother and father, mother suddenly asked whether I had found the meaning of repeating obeisance five times. I confessed that I had not. She replied" Goddess exists in all elements and every thing is made of five elements hence obeisance is paid five times.

With preponderance of demonical characteristics in the world, rampant with corruption. The greed, lust and anger having its sway let us rededicate ourselves to goddess Durga to help us in killing demons in us and free our mind from confusion and attain success & grace in our life.

*Comments attached*

# 62. GO CRAZY

MUCK

When everything around is spotlessly clean, it does not make us happy. we require a bit of dirt - our own everyday stink to enjoy and excel in performance, production, pay & promotion 4P. We also develop our own muck in order to enjoy family, friend, fun and festival 4F.

CRAZE

Like a fish without water, human being devoid of these 4p & 4f is not comfortable unless you develop a craze - this craze may be for any physical, mental or spiritual entity. This madness is so strong and invisible - only you & near ones are affected. You like other to emulate it and are disturbed when they fail to be mad. you are happy when you are crazy, no social rule affects you.

ENLIGHTENMENT

Go crazy -nothing can be achieved without craziness – not even Enlightenment.

*Comments attached*

# 63. HELP

Help that is given as a matter of duty,
To a deserving candidate
At the right place and time,
Is true help full of compassion.
Help that is given unwillingly,
Or to get something in return,
Or looking for some fruit,
Is not help but business.
Help that is given at a wrong place and time,
To unworthy persons, without paying respect
Or with contempt, is said to be an insult.,
Never help a fully fit young man begging
But curse the man who made him a beggar.
As a teacher, never provide solution to a problem
 But help him figure it out himself.
You cannot help anyone who does not ask for it.
Proving the theory that you are God of your world.
Help is always available when you look for it.
You look for doctor when you are sick.
You look for a carpenter to mend your chair.
You look for a plumber to repair your pipes.
You look for a service provider for a service
You look for a religion based on your propensities
You look within yourself to develop spirituality.
External world is full of delusion
Internal world provides you illumination
Your physical and mental strength deplete in delusion
Where shall you find it for achieving illumination.
So seek help now, make the commitment
Life bird is on its wing shall leave your domain.

## 64. HONOR & DIGNITY

Honor and dignity is slaughtered before a few golden grains. Many a battle has been fought for honor and dignity of nation. There may be honor amongst the thieves but there is none in police, people who shy away from work, where is the dignity of labor. A veiled prostitute looses her dignity as soon as she is recognized. In a country where every man has become a broker Every product being sold to highest bidder, every rule flouted in the name justice, where human life has no price. where every effort is made to earn a few rupee more. Then where is honor where is dignity. Politics are swayed by criminals, teaching is lost in corruption. Administration is lost in procrastination and justice is more inclined to sensational

Gone are the days when man died for ashes of father and temple of god. Gone are the days of chivalry – honor and gallantry. Gone are the days when your own safety, honor and welfare came last always and every time. Gone are the days of Joint family where harmony existed. Gone are the days where honor and dignity lay in sacrifices.

Today temple of Gods are commercial establishment, ashes of father a mere pollution, Today gender equality is stressed denying the ladies their due respect. Today gratification of own need, safety and welfare reign supreme. Basic human behavior based on sacrifice has got corrupted and an attitude of indifference has set in. The honor and dignity is at its nadir. It does not affect a spiritual man, for him the honor and dishonor has no meaning.

*Comments attached*

# 65. MAN REMAIN CALM

Watch don't react, be calm
Agitated mind does not sing psalm.
I pondered when man remain calm
Inspite of provocation, he is mum.

He is endowed with calmness by nature
He is outwardly controlling his emotion
Dwelling on retaliation at right occasion.
He doesnot understand the situation.
He finds it profitable to remain calm.
He may have some axe to grind.

He is coaxed by ritual or power to keep mum
He may be blackmailed to observe silence
He may be heavily bribed to keep quite
He may have been threatened to keep his cool
His action may be detrimental to his welfare
These may be real or he assumes it so.

The action and reactions are in confrontation
There is no temporal change during condensation
All passion and delusion are led to termination
- when a man contemplate self realization

# 66. MANS HAPPINESS LIES WITH THE MAN

A bit of companionship
Sharing bit of emotion
A bit of recognition
A bit of involvement
A bit of caring
A bit of stroking
A bit of attention
A bit of obedience
A bit of ego boosting
And man is oozing happiness.

When there is no dream of companionship
Emotion has no place and respect false
Carrot and stick in lieu of recognition
Involvement is not truly appreciated
Caring, sharing and stroking prohibited
Always obeying the diktat is detrimental.

Yet I am happy and I have no complain
 It was my choice that is truth plain.
so choose mindfully and you would be happy

*Comments attached*

# 67. MONKEY KING

All the animals in the forest concluded that the lion was ferocious and could provide security from poacher from other jungle animals but would eat some animal occasionally, they then decided that monkey be chosen to be the king. After a few days the goat mother came running to the Monkey King that her kid has been captured by the lion. Monkey immediately sprang into action, jumping from one tree to another threw branches and stones on the lion.

Lion was not bothered, ate the goat, the goat mother cried that she lost her kid. The monkey said "was there any lack of effort from my side, see the perspiration, I cannot be blamed for loss of your kid.

This is what happens when you place your trust on incompetent person. In spite of hard work you don't succeed in your mission. Napoleon had said

'If a person is intelligent and lazy he shall go to the top.

If he is intelligent and hardworking he will be in the middle

If he is foolish and lazy you can employ him grade 3 or 4.

But if he is foolish and hardworking, shoot him- because you don't know what Chaos he may create.

In the path of realization, excessive rituals are a barrier to enlightenment. When you place your trust on Ego, light of your soul is eclipsed. So riding on your animalistic propensities, gaining multiple competencies subdue the Ego and your success in every domain is Guaranteed. Excessive ritual can be identified as monkey King it cannot save your soul for communion with the God.

*Comments attached*

## 68. WHAT BRINGS HAPPINESS?

It is not satisfaction of ego,
But eternal compromise between what you clasp and forgo.
When you realize interaction of sacrifice and love
 Find their correlation limited to a personification
If material wealth is discounted life is miserable
What brings happiness is human relationship.
You sacrifice human relationship at alter of your ego
 Intellect rises, mind numbed, heart races but system fails
Physical and mental health deteriorate,
Emotional fulfillment a rarity,
You now have a constipated look
 and your personality degrades.
You are stranger in your family
 In spite of respect for the old
And affection for the young
You become a demi god.
Your progeny are psychologically cripple
Your wife spend time in frivolous activities
 Life continues reducing status to non doer ship
This is the fruit you bear for upward mobility

# 69. PEACE AND HARMONY REIGN IN UNISON

A child cries when its doll is snatch
It cannot weigh pros or cons
For him sole possession is his doll
 No other alternative consoles him
You are entangled in lust and anger
No other thought flash in your mind
For you, communion with lord is sad
I feel sad for your shortsightedness.
Human life with mindboggling intelligence
Is something much more than natural instinct
What have you done with all that is given
 Nothing, you are thief in your mind.
 There are murderer who have not yet murdered
There are rapist who are yet to rape
There are lot of criminals yet to commit crime
There are lot of potential which are to be exploited,
Get above your body and mind
Put little effort and you shall find
Infatuation beyond expectation
Love and joy beyond imagination.
All suffering led to extinction
Conscience expanded beyond horizon
Notice to all thought for eviction
Peace and harmony reign in unison.

*Comments attached*

# 70. PERCEIVED TRAITS AND POSSIBLE OUTCOMES

Resolved to adorn myself with
Shield of honesty and Truth
Keep corruption and falsehood at bay
Heavy club of extensive knowledge
Keep vanity and ignorance away.

Sharp sword of discrimination
Cutting across hypocrisy and glamour
Trident of physical, mental and spiritual wisdom
Keep my mind from infatuation of women and wealth

Sharp arrow of intelligence
To fight the forces of dark and evil.
Disc of universal compassion
To get rid of derisive and communal forces

Balm of love and affection
Keep my ego at the minimum.
Thunder of body strength
Keeping free of disease and misery

My consciousness is expanding endlessly
Success ensured in every field
After three score years I remain
Unattached friend and guide to all.
With essential support of woman and wealth
There is no one to disturb my state of happiness
I am content in self and lost in the Self.
With no yearning or striving pass away one day.

*Comments attached*

# 71. RADHA - PRINCESS OF BEAUTY AND GRACE

'Madhurādhi-pater akhilaṁ madhuram' is said about lord Krishna. same attribute on Radha would appear thus

1) Her lips are lovely, Her face is lovely Her eyes are lovely,

   Her smile is lovely, heart is lovely, Her gait is lovely—
   Everything is lovely about the Princess of beauty and grace!

2) Her words are lovely, Her character is lovely Her dress is lovely,

   Her belly-folds are lovely, Her movements are lovely, Her wandering is lovely —Everything is lovely about the Princess of beauty and grace!

3) Her flute is lovely, Her foot-dust is lovely Her hands are lovely,

   Her feet are lovely, Her dancing is lovely, Her friendship is lovely—
   Everything is lovely about the Princess of beauty and grace!

4) Her singing is lovely, Her blue cloth is lovely, Her eating is lovely,

   Her sleeping is lovely,Her beauty is lovely, Her tilaka is lovely —Everything is lovely about the Princess of beauty and grace!

5) Her deeds are lovely,Her liberating is lovely, Her stealing is lovely,

   Her love-sports are lovely Her oblations are lovely, Her tranquility is lovely—Everything is lovely about the Princess of beauty and grace!

6) Her gunja-berry necklace is lovely, Her flower garland is lovely Her Yamuna river is lovely, Her ripples are lovely, Her water is lovely,

   Her lotuses are lovely
   —Everything is lovely about the Princess of beauty and grace!

7) Her gopas are lovely,Her pastimes are lovely, Her union is lovely,

Her food is lovely, Her delight is lovely, Her courtesy is lovely — Everything is lovely about the Princess of beauty and grace!

8) Her gopis are lovely, Her cows are lovely Her staff is lovely,

Her creation is lovely Her trampling is lovely, Her fruitfulness is lovely
—Everything is lovely about the Princess of beauty and grace!

*Comments attached*

# 72. RAINY DAY ANTS TAUGHT ME

It was month of June, I was looking at the evening sky where dark clouds were gathering for the first rain of the season. There was hushed silence indicating impending downpour. On ground rows and rows of ants, big strong ones were lining up emerging from the ant hill, they were not moving anywhere but seemed to be waiting. Then big drops of rain were spattering being sucked by the hungry earth. It rained for a hour or so. What do I see on the ground, the rows of ants have got scattered and wings are spouting on their back.

Frolicking

Before long they start flying in utter freedom and joy. The female flying faster than the smaller drones. They are making love all night. In the morning you see some dead drones surrounded by some wings. Tired of love making and shorn of her wing she had crawled back to the ant hill. My heart was heavy for the dead ants who bravely and patiently waited for rain to sprouting of their wings, frolicking all night Knowing fully well that they shall meet their end by the morning.

Time fly by trying to achieve excellence

We also wait patiently for result of examination, carry out passing out parade for commission. We wait for excellence in physical, mental and spiritual domain. We see time fly by trying to achieve excellence, very soon we feel redundant. We like ants procreate to make human life immortal

Peril of life

Nature is great in economy once an entity becomes redundant, it is eliminated. Life of ants shall help us in leading a free and fearless life. Metamorphosis in life is assured. So earn your wings and discharge your duties at the peril of your life. That is the only way to live.

*Comments attached*

# 73. SALVATION FROM SIN

All major religion promises salvation from sin as an ultimate goal. Human being have inbuilt soul which are in two states, one divine and other demonical. We also accept that modes of nature play dominant role in the physical state of human being.

Now what is Sin?

The seven deadly sins, (Lust, greed, anger, envy, pride, sloth and gluttony) reside in the EGO of the being, it can be looked as policy manager of the mind and can veto the decision of the intellect. No action is sin, it is the intention that makes it so. Sin is said to break Gods law and not law of the land. So no legal action can be taken against sin, only you can atone them. All religion agree that sin arises from uncontrolled lust greed and anger. some of which are Adultery, stealing, killing, bearing false witness.

Modus operandi for providing salvation.

For souls with divine State. You shall be free of sins if your mind is cleansed. let us see how 1. Surrendering :Lord Krishna advises Arjun to leave aside all righteous deeds and surrender to him. When you surrender you loose your Ego, With it you also loose your Sins. You are no more doer only an outward cause.

GRACE OF LORD

1    Grace of Lord : A person cultivating Christian value of humility only requires Grace of lord to have his ego wiped out. Jesus rightly said you obey ten commandments and inculcate 10 virtues you can be sure of getting rid of the sins.

MERCY

2.   Gaining Mercy : Mohammad said if with devotion you ask Allah for forgiveness, He shall surely have mercy on you and pardon your sins.

3.   Enlightenment : You achieve enlightenment when your Intellect is in communion with your soul, ego gets by passed and with enlightenment you achieve salvation.

Soul in demonical self

Souls in demonic state. Souls in demonic state do not believe in surrender, or forgiveness. Their life is full of lust. greed and anger. They demonstrate their power and strength. They believe in physical and mental state only. They claim ' I am rich and well born, who else is equal to me. I will sacrifice, I will give alms and I will rejoice'. ' this enemy is slain by me today, others shall also be slain. I am Lord. I enjoy, I am successful and happy.' Souls in divine state are their enemies. They seek no salvation

No sin in Spiritual domain

The modes of nature ( goodness, passion and delusion ) hides the soul. The physical and mental state are governed by combination of modes. This is where sins are defined. There are no sin in spiritual domain. you realise Self in self

*Comments attached*

# 75. SMILE PLEASE

A kid's smile fills your heart
 A youth smiles in anticipation
A man smile when his scheme of things works
An old man smiles knowing the consequence.
A girl smile when demands are met
A women smile to incite her suitor
An old women smile when her planning works
A women of the world smiles on her gain
All people smile when they are pleased
Smile on what you think is yours
Smile when you are found out
Smile when you keep it secret
 Smile when you encourage others
 Smile when you admonish someone.

Smile at the birth of issues and ideas
Smile at love legitimate and impromptu
Smile at friendship real or virtual
Smile at simple and complicated situation
Smile when defeated partially and wholly
Smile when victorious by fair or foul means
Smile on yourself and your limitation
Smile continues till your journey is done.

*Comments attached*

# 75. SUCCESS PRINCIPLES IN PHYSICAL AND SPIRITUAL DOMAIN ARE SAME

1. Success principles are the same whether you are trying to succeed at work, in your relationship or with your wealth or at being realized soul. 1. Knowledge - Know what you want-set Aim &Aim-plus You must have the desire to succeed. This means you need to know what you want in life and be able to identify the actions that you need to take to achieve your goals. But Thou shalt not kill, Jesus commands.

2. Proactive Action – develop competencies - Never give up It's easy for people to become disheartened when they are criticised or encounter a hurdle while trying to achieve their goals, but to be a true success you must persist through the criticism, rejection, pressure and failure. A fighting spirit will make you succeed. Persistence is the number one thing for being successful

3. Devotion to duty - Believe in yourself To be successful you need to have a positive outlook and believe that you can achieve your goals. When you feel good about yourself, you react more confidently to life's challenges. If you believe in yourself and push yourself through shyness and self-doubt you will succeed more far than you will fail. Believe and you will achieve. Jesus commands I am the LORD thy God Thou shalt have no other gods No graven images or likenesses Not take the LORD's name in vain He means Believe in yourself.

4. Never stop learning- you mind matures with learning process Unless you update you are outdated, Successful people never stop learning. They learn from their mistakes, new experiences and other people. Learning at every opportunity increases your knowledge in old and new areas and keeps you ahead in your field. Honour thy father and thy mother, your learning never ends

5. Surrender to your goal - Do what you love Remember the sabbath day. Jesus commands. Being passionate about the things you spend your time on is energizing and motivates you to succeed. Do what you love, and success will come.

6. Realization - Avoid conditional happiness to be happy Some of conditional happiness Jesus prohibited Thou shalt not commit adultery Thou shalt not steal Thou shalt not bear false witness Thou shalt not covet Happiness is a state of mind you can be happy at any place at any time Success shall follow you in all walks of life in the hills or the vines.

*Comments attached*

## 76. THIS IS ENJOYMENT

Every day a present,
or wonder where it went..........
Enjoy pain and pleasure
heaven or hell whatever
Morning so pleasant
bed so comfortable
accepting the gift glowing pink
back to slumber, obnoxious brink.
Hurriedly completing shit, shave and shampoo,
Negotiating breakfast in a record time
Ready for road with briefcase and what have you
But road is agonizingly slow to your work place.
Everyone want the job done as of yesterday
There are number of aspirant to take your place
Day and part of night lost in coffee and office gossip
Daily complaint from family ringing in your ear
You go to sleep, reading a book, without any fear.
Oh Lord where is the time for enjoyment?
And Lord said 'this is enjoyment, my dear.'

## 77. YARDSTICK IS VARIABLE

Everybody has a yardstick
Measuring others by it
Each value is measured by it
Tolerance level is noted carefully.`
Ideally yardstick is based on
Natural justice, fair play & good faith.
But it gets corrupted as
Justice is will of strong on the weak
Everything is fair in love and war
All faith are good unless proved otherwise.
You fall in your eyes is yardstick
Your conscience pricks you
Benefit accrued is never
Commensurate with loss of yardstick
You become weather cock
Changing as the wind blows.
It is good to loose your yardstick
Experience gained make it better.
I also had a strong yardstick
I had no friend really
As none would measure to it
Some failed in truthfulness
Some were full of deception
Some had no moral courage
Some were too earthy
Some were too intellectual
Some were too rich
Some only took advantage
Some delighted in mischief
Some played office politics
Some did not match chemistry
I became a snob
Everybody rejected me
I lowered my yardstick
Yet I could not match.

Some called me mad
Some called me proud
Some would call me unsocial
Though it was not true.
Let my friends amass wealth
Let them overtake me
My yardstick is unchanged
Lord- only you measure to it
We all have some yardstick or
Terms of reference as some call it
Our value of life depends on it
Our success or failure results from it.
This yardstick is held very secret
As emotional state depends on it
Yet this yardstick compels us
To measure against actual state
Sometime we are left wanting
Sometime we are overwhelmed by it.
Our fundamental values may be truth,
Honesty, justice fairplay and good faith
But to climb social ladder they change to
Make belief, hypocrisy and selfishness.

*Comments attached*

## 78.   CREATE YOUR SMALL WORLD

You can be as bad as you want
 Beset with harming people without respite
It is your venom that is burning you
It does not affect rest of the world.

You can be as good as you want
You may get mercilessly harmed by others
You do not waver from your path
You gain vanity without affecting others

People may pay obeisance in fear
 Or respect you as benevolent savior
When you pass away or are eliminated
World continues as usual unaffected.

 You may get help from like minded
When you paint win-win situation
All the fine mansion you build
Shall reduce to rubble as time passes

You shall reap interest on your investment
If you invest in wealth you reap wealth
If you invest in human you reap attachment
 All other wealth are useless as time passes

 O seeker of pleasure shunning pain
Your tradeoff is unbalanced gain
Time evens up pleasure and pain
Working ceaselessly die in harness.

In your small world do bring in cheer
Let smile greet you, eyes show no fear.

*Comments attached*

# COMMENTS AND RESPONSES BY SEEKERS AMD MASTERS OF SPEAKING TREE TOI

## BOOK V.
## RANDOM RESULTS OF HARMONY OF LIFE AND MIND

### 55. .A POOR MAN LIKE ME FULL OF FEAR

***Dayakrishan Mehrotra***
*I like the slide as it is very divine blog and I feel that there is no reason of fear to devotee of God LORD KRISHNA. JAI SHRI KRISHNA !!!!!*

***Somnath Banerjee in reply to Dayakrishan Mehrot...***
*Jai shri Krishna, fear then vanishes my dear*

***Amiya Basu***
*Very nice Somnath Babu. Some more poems please.*

***Somnath Banerjee in reply to Amiya Basu***
*Thanks, you may read my book Introspection" Auther house*

***Muralidhar Gopalan***
*Sir, really heart touching lines*

***Somnath Banerjee in reply to Muralidhar Gopalan***
*It is not heart but mind*
*thanks*

***Sham Lal Mehta***
*When HE is there*
*Nothing to fear*
*In this world here*
*of nether worlds there.*

*God Bless you, Sir.*

***Somnath Banerjee in reply to Sham Lal Mehta***
*THANKS,*

## 57. BETTER HUMAN BEING

### Arun Laha
*Sufferings, bestowed by Almighty, teach us lessons; I had personal experience; I have empathy for you; pray to Almighty for your well-being; think about the Rabindrasangit - "AJI JHARAR RATE TOMAR ABHISAR".*
*Reply*

### Somnath Banerjee in reply to Arun Laha
*Thanks. my submission is that you become a better human being.*

### Shri Dattaswami
*God created this world with both happy and unhappy situations in altering fashion. Summer is followed by winter, and winter is again followed by summer. Day is followed by night and night is followed by day. This world is created for the entertainment of God in the ultimate sense. The sweet and hot dishes are prepared in the palace for the king. You are only a guest joining the king in the meals. The king is enjoying both the sweet and hot dishes equally. If you are enjoying only sweets and reluctant to the hot dishes, you are only a child and you are not the grown up adult like the king to enjoy both the dishes equally. You cannot be equal to the king in having the power of the administration of the kingdom. That point is ruled out. If you can enjoy the sweet and hot dishes equally like the king, you can become equal to king at least in this one concept of eating. If you behave like a child and become reluctant to the hot dishes you are in no way equal to the king in any angle. Similarly, you have no power of creation, control and destruction of this world like God. You cannot be equal to God in these angles. If you become equal to God in enjoying both happy and unhappy situations, you can be claimed to be equal to God at least in this one angle.*

*You should not say that God is only spectator and not involved in the world directly. God is involved in the world through human incarnation like Rama, Krishna etc. as any human being is involved. The word Rama means the continuous enjoyment through continuous entertainment. If you see the life of Rama, there were several tragic scenes. Rama wept when His wife Sita was stolen. He was internally enjoying while weeping externally. This is similar to internal enjoyment of hot dish by an adult in whom you find the external signs of weeping only. It is said that Rama gives the salvation while alive (Jeevanmukti). The word Rama is said to be taraka mantra, which means that you will cross the grief. Grief is inevitable in the life. How to cross it? You can cross it only by learning the technique of enjoying it. Without understanding this meaning of the word Rama, there will be no use of chanting the word Rama continuously.*

*At this level of this concept, the difference between good and bad also vanishes as said in Gita (Buddhi Yukto Jahatiha...). Rama wept when His wife was stolen. The reason for this grief was the result of a bad action performed by Him previously as Lord Vishnu. Lord Vishnu killed the wife of sage Bhrugu. The present grief is the result of that previous sin. But, still, Rama enjoyed the grief internally so that He is always in the continuous state of entertainment and enjoyment only. Hence, this concept is the state of highest philosophy. This alone can be the real and permanent solution to be in constant state of bliss in which the stress and strain cannot exist at any time.*

*Mr. Anil asked that whether this will encourage the sin. Swami replied: You need not fear for this because in this state there is no interest in doing some wrong action for selfish benefit. When you can enjoy the state of absence of selfish benefit also, where is the need for doing sin? Sin is said to be the wrong action performed for selfish benefit. Lord Vishnu also killed the wife of sage Bhrugu, since she was protecting a demon, who is harmful to the world. There was no selfishness in that action, but, the sage Bhrugu cursed Lord Vishnu due to his emotional ignorance. This curse can be actually nullified since there was no sin in reality. But the Lord welcomed it since He is fond of grief as an interval dish. Hence in this level of the divine state of God, there cannot be any possibility of even a trace of sin. The source of sin is selfishness and there is no need of selfishness in this state since self and non-self are equally enjoyed.*

**Somnath Banerjee in reply to Shri Dattaswami**
*Your comment though out of context is accepted and noted*

*ENJOY PAIN ENJOY PLEASURE - enjoyment is continuous.*

**Shri Dattaswami in reply to Somnath Banerjee**

*There are several illustrations to prove that the physical pain can be also enjoyed. In boxing, when the opponent embraces you strongly, you feel unhappy because such a situation leads to your defeat. But, when you are embraced by a beautiful girl, you feel more happiness and the degree of your happiness is proportional to the strength of the embracement!. Therefore, the physical pain in one situation is unhappy, whereas the same physical pain in another situation leads to happiness. Even when you eat the hot dish, your tongue is burning due to the vigor of chillies and your eyes are showering the tears. All these symptoms are the indication of unhappiness only.*

*But still you enjoy the happiness in eating the hot dish. Therefore, you cannot link the enjoyment with mere external material. Ofcourse, the external material gives rise to the feeling and the feeling may be pleasant or unpleasant depending on one factor, which is that whether the external material is interacted continuously or not. If you are interacting with any item or situation of the creation continuously, you become unhappy. Even the embracement of the beautiful girl becomes unpleasant, if such embracement continues without gap.*

*If you are exposed to the heat for a long time you feel happiness in cold as in the case of the Indian. If you are exposed to cold for a long time you feel happiness in the warmness and heat as in the case of a foreigner. Hence the process of enjoyment depends on the alternating interaction with the external items or situations in this world. Hence, any continuous interaction with the same item or situation gives unhappiness, whereas the change in the interaction gives happiness. God is the Father of the souls and hence arranges the life cycles of the souls with alternating pleasant and unpleasant scenes.*

*Even though you have done sins continuously for some long span of time and good deeds continuously in another long span of time, God does not arrange the life cycles with the continuous misery and continuous happiness proportionally in corresponding long spans of time.*

*God neglects this continuous span of time and arranges the life cycle in such a way so that every life cycle is fixed with alternating fruits of sins and good deeds. The re-arrangement of the good and bad fruits in alternating fashion by drawing good and bad fruits from both these span is done by God, who is omnipotent.*

*You may expect God to cancel all the sins due to His omnipotent nature. If it is done like that, you will not enjoy since continuity of anything leads to misery. Hence even in such case, misery is inevitable. Therefore, if you do not pray God for removing the miseries, God has already arranged the life cycles in best way to give you continuous enjoyment. You are praying God to remove the difficulties, which are the fruits of your bad deeds. The law of justice does not accept the cancellation of the fruit of any deed. Hence, due to your prayers the difficulties are postponed to later births by God along with compounded interest. You also pray God to give continuous happiness. For this God, draws the good fruits from the future births with reduced interest to the present life cycle. Due to such continuous enjoyment of good fruits, you are again bored with misery.*

*Hence, you are totally foolish in disturbing the already designed life cycles of God. As a result of this foolishness your future births will be full of continuous miseries. The continuity of the misery gives you unhappiness just like the continuity of happiness. Therefore, pray God always attracted by your love to His divine personality and not for disturbing the already best designed life cycles by God due to His paternal affection. Therefore, you will be continuously happy by enjoying the alternating pleasant and unpleasant scenes of life and by not asking anything from God.*

*www.universal-spirituality.org*
*Universal Spirituality for World Peace*

**Somnath Banerjee in reply to Shri Dattaswami**
*It is a matter of concern that you are having fatalistic and escapist attitude towards sins and virtues, pleasure and pain.*

*There is choice offered to man one born out of consciousness i.e. ego and conscience, your choice leads to results sometime pleasant sometime painful. the choice also depends on interaction of consciousness both logic and emotion participating in the ambient condition.*

*Oh God in human form uncondition your mind, let there be union of consciousness with conscience. this is universal spirituality.*

**Arun Laha in reply to Somnath Banerjee**
*'Experience pain-and-pleasure of this material plane as dispassionate observer' - ancient Indian wisdom teaches us this lesson for smooth sailing in our worldly life.*

**Somnath Banerjee in reply to Arun Laha**
*It is possible when equamity is attained.*
*i do not doubt wisdom.*
*long time no see*

**Shri Dattaswami**
*One need not run away from the problems*

*The devotee can become the Lord in all aspects except the aspect of creation, maintenance and destruction of universe. The other aspects are not at all disturbed due to absence of the last aspect. Suppose a producer of a film is enjoying His own picture. Though you are not the producer, you can enjoy the cinema in equal status with the producer. You can enjoy just like the producer because you are enjoying the same cinema without taking the laborious efforts of its production. Therefore you should not say that since he is the producer, he is enjoying.*

*People often say that since the human incarnation is Lord, He can enjoy the tragic scenes of the cinema. Do you mean that the producer only can enjoy the tragic scenes of the cinema? Any spectator can enjoy the tragic scenes of the cinema. The only requirement for such continuous enjoyment of comic and tragic scenes of the cinema is only the realization of the nature of the cinema. If you know that the cinema is unreal, you can enjoy even the tragic scene.*

*Whether the spectator is a producer of the film or an ordinary human being the requirement for the continuous enjoyment of the cinema is only the knowledge about the unreality of the cinema. Therefore you need not run away from the problems of the life and leaving the theater is committing suicide. Therefore do not say that Rama, Krishna etc are God and so could stand unperturbed during the difficult times in life. The argument is completely wrong and what you lack is the knowledge of the reality of this creation (forms and feelings) and not the producer-ship of this creation.*

*www.universal-spirituality.org*
*Universal Spirituality for World Peace*

### Somnath Banerjee in reply to Shri Dattaswami
*One need not run away from the problems. Problems are challenges that you face. A soldier takes the bullet in the chest and not in the back. A Soldier of lord faces all calamity with equamity having surrendered to his Loving mate.*

*The devotee can become the Lord in all aspects except the aspect of creation, maintenance and destruction of universe.*

*Sorry, you are the God of your universe. All attributes and functions of your universe is defined in your mind, you don't believe or recognize any other universe. You agree that*

*People often say that since the human incarnation is Lord,*

*You develop Krishna consciousness in your mind, then you would be able to fight all the aushuras with ease.*

### Abc Narayan
*Most realistic and impressive poem.*

*And, Becoming 'better human and full surrender'.*

### Somnath Banerjee in reply to Abc Narayan
*Thanks, there is no alternative, without faith in Almighty you cannot withstand the pain and sufferings*

### Col Gurnam Singh
*Wishing you all the best with your recovery. May you use this restful time to recharge and energize. All the best.*

### Somnath Banerjee in reply to Col Gurnam Singh
*Thanks for your kind wishes.*

*Metabolism is a life function normally has two phases anabolic and ketabolic,-.at this stage of life recharging is very slow, one has to accept what nature returns.*

### Col Gurnam Singh in reply to Somnath Banerjee
*I agree.*

### Somnath Banerjee in reply to Col Gurnam Singh
*Welcome*

## 59. BODY GLOW

**Dr**
*Meaningful, very good lines :*
*Cool water in leaky tub is caressing*
*You did nothing but continued sleeping*
*On reaching nose it is suffocating*
*Frenzy action yet you are sinking*
*A good attempt to wake up the sleeping ones.*
*But there are millions and millions wide awake and rushing fast to doom.*
*They are self-declaired wise, self- esteemed who listen to none except the one like them only.*
*They have no idea of heaven and have accepted ' The Hell ' as their heaven and happy with their lot.*
*They are the leader, they are the masses, they are the preacher and they are the teacher.*
*You have made a nice attempt. Let us hope for something better. ..*
*Regards.*

**Somnath Banerjee in reply to Dr**
*No one can awaken you except yourself,*
*It is valid for all irrespective of space, time and consciousness.*

**Dr in reply to Somnath Banerjee**
*Exactly. Only those can be awakened who are willing to. That too by one self only.*
*Regards.*

**Somnath Banerjee in reply to Dr**
*See my next blog being custodian dont act like owner '*

**Dr in reply to Somnath Banerjee**
*Sure.*
*Thanks.*

**Prakash Chavan**
*Body glow comes from glow within. Beautiful saying. But in spiritual elevation we will have to go beyond body*
*Regards.*

**Somnath Banerjee in reply to Prakash Chavan**
*Your face is index of mind. body glow of a fair maiden in love and
a holy man in meditation are different
one affects your gonads and the other the pineal (crown chakra,)*

## 60. CAN YOU JUSTIFY DECEPTION AS RELIGION

**Sunita Gupta**
*So votaries of deception can you justify deception as religion... no
religion says that but men use religion to promote their own interest !*

**Somnath Banerjee in reply to Sunita Gupta**
*So madame you are saying that deception is part of every religion.
does spirituality tolerate deception.*

**Sunita Gupta in reply to Somnath Banerjee**
*OMG... !! deception is not part of any religion. all religions are
very clear about what to do ; what not to do ; how to live. .... !*

**Somnath Banerjee in reply to Sunita Gupta**
*Agreed, bible (mat 5.3) says your right hand should not know what
your left hand is doing.
in Mahabharata it is full of deception.
Muhammad allows deception in koran,
all tycoons are full of deception without exception.
You have a conscience which tells you what to do and what not to
do why religion is required.
Anmol Sharma
Good work*

**Somnath Banerjee in reply to Anmol Sharma**
*Thanks*

**Anmol Sharma**
*Good work*

## 61. DURGA – CONFUSION TERMINATOR

**Saroj Das**
*Five time repeating symbolizes the five elements and every thing is
made of five elements. Agreed. Have you any clue as to how these
five elements are made or created?*

**Somnath Banerjee in reply to Saroj Das**
*These five elements vary with religion and religion it can be looked up in google. According to me these are solid, liquid, gases associated with time and space. the matter (solid liquid and gases) is made from the same elementary particles, h/Time gives you energy. Hinduism has correlated Solid as earth,liquid as water, gas as air, fire as energy and ether as space.*
*Thank you*

**Saroj Das in reply to Somnath Banerjee**
*Thanks. However, i beg to disagree that elements vary with religion. H2O should be universally water. i am trying to brief about elements, as understood by scholars of Hindu philosophy. If you may like to know how the universe comes in to existence (a scientific explanation) according to Vedanta, i can provide.*

*Matter in its gross form has five states and in its subtle form has five qualities known as sense objects in tne vedic texts.There are five inlets and also five outlets located in the human body; thus twenty in total.The five states of the gross matter are space, air, fire, water and earth and in their subtle form they are the sound, touch, sight, taste and smell respectively.The inlets are the ears,skin, eyes, tongue and the nose of which the outlets are the vocal cord, hands, legs,genital and anus respectively.The grossest matter is the earth, having all the five qualities in it. It can be smelt, tasted, seen, touched and heard. Water has four qualities; it can not be smelt. Fire has three; it can not be tasted, air has two; it can not be seen and finally space; which can not be touched.The world of perception and action becomes possible only with the active participation of the mind; the twentyfirst.It does not matter whether the sense organs alongwith the mind are evolved products of inert matter or the universe is an imagination of the mind. But, since the existence of sound can not be established with out establishing the existence of the ear, they must coexist. Word co exists with God! "First there was God, and Word was with God. Therefore, Word, verily is God". (Bible).*

**Somnath Banerjee in reply to Saroj Das**
*Thank you for your kind briefing. Though the elements do not vary, some are more fundamental than other*

**Classical Elements**
*Babylonian Earth,Sea, Wind, Sky, Fire*
*Greek........Air,Water, ether,Fire,Earth*
*Hinduism (Tattva),Buddhism (Mahābhūta), Jainism (Tattva)*
*Vayu, Ap, Akasha, Agni,prithvi*
*Chinese (Wuxing) Wood, Water Earth Fire Metal*
*Japanese (Godai) Air,Water Void, Fire, Earth*
*Tibetan (Bön) Air,WaterAetherFireEarth*
*Medieval Alchemy Air, Water AetherFire Earth Sulphur MercurySalt*
*buddhism consider only four leaving space this i got from google*

**Saroj Das in reply to Somnath Banerjee**
*Mind is Matter, and 'pleasure and pain' are it's modifications! (Geeta ch.13). Thanks. How the mind becomes the Universe? Regards.*

## 62. GO CRAZY

**Shekhar Ray**
*Go crazy to destroy yourself*
*and thus discover the new one in you !*

**Somnath Banerjee in reply to Shekhar Ray**
*Anyway be crazy- keeps you away from distractions,*
*Creation and destruction is illusion- are you crazy enough to feel this*

## 64. HONOR & DIGNITY

**Sharda Prabhakar**
*Current scenario very well expressed. But spiritual or not,values hold their value anytime everytime and to everyone.*

**Somnath Banerjee in reply to Sharda Prabhakar**
*When you have minimized your Ego, transcended modes of nature, your values undergo change you are unaffected (gita ch2)*

**Sharda Prabhakar in reply to Somnath Banerjee**
*Forums like these with such enlightening articles might inspire us to get on this path.Thanq*

*I am at the very beginning of the journey but I do share similar thoughts as far as ego is concerned.http://www.speakingtree.in/ public/spiritual-blogs/ seekers/science-of-spirituality/on-handling-humili ation*

### Somnath Banerjee in reply to Sharda Prabhakar

*When you are humiliated your ego grows stronger. your honor and dignity is unaffected, it is quite possible he is hiding his weakness or lacks upbringing*

### Sunita Gupta

*That is whaer when you reach --you can witness all without seething inside but then satva is also part of your atma--how long you can be inert ?*

### Somnath Banerjee in reply to Sunita Gupta

*Very wise comment!*
*life is kinetic, as gita states Lord is also active all the time. may appear inert sometime.*

### Sunita Gupta in reply to Somnath Banerjee

*Uski baatein woh hi jaane !*

### Somnath Banerjee in reply to Sunita Gupta

*As we are puppet of lord, we should atleast understand ourself.*
**Shekhar Ray** *Although you have said all bitter truths, degradation of social structure but there is no other way so we have to remain with our positive hope... with our faith on God. .... all is well. ... all is well !*

### Somnath Banerjee in reply to Shekhar Ray

*Courage, brother, do not stumble,*
*Though thy path is dark as night;*
*There's a star to guide the humble--*
*Trust in God and do the right.*

*God does not interfere the evolution process. my lament is loss of honor and dignity, knowing fully well a spiritual person should be above this*

## 66. MANS HAPPINESS LIES WITH THE MAN

### Harcharan Lamba
*Sir, Spirituality is a practical path of love. When we walk on spiritual path and progress within we experience divine happiness, peace and bliss. There are no adequate words to describe bliss.*

*However, would request to revisit the blog: "The Greatest Happiness" which are words of true living Master for further insight.*

### Somnath Banerjee in reply to Harcharan Lamba
*I do not doubt the words of living or nonliving masters, they are all correct. the attributes of soul are divine and demoniacal, both draw strength from spiritual process. do both get bliss*

### Harcharan Lamba in reply to Somnath Banerjee
*What is demoniacal is duality (of mind-matter) that it it gets entrapped into.*

### Somnath Banerjee in reply to Harcharan Lamba
*Gita chapter 16*

### Harcharan Lamba
*The true happiness lies within each of us. We just need to invert within to connect with the ocean of divine love for permanent peace and bliss.*
*Would request to visit my blog: "The Greatest Happiness" for further insight.*

### Somnath Banerjee in reply to Harcharan Lamba
*What you say is true.*
*you have to stop bubbles in your mind and you are in bliss unaffected by ambient condition,*
*see my blog you can be happy anywhere at any time.*
*i have not understood'invert within' what are you inverting.*

### Harcharan Lamba in reply to Somnath Banerjee
*Yes, stopping the bubbles/waves of mind are very important. For that we need to invert within means to go within, sitting in deep silence, meditation to connect the source of all joy and bliss, which lies within each of us.*

*Somnath Banerjee in reply to Harcharan Lamba*
*The emotion joy and bliss are in different complexes in the brain so are the other logic and emotion, how do you reach the source of bliss*

*Prakash Chavan*
*When you are happy why I should feel jealous. This is natural attitude of man. When somebody is happy we wear mask to show him that he has become happy but the undercurrent is of jealousy. So mans happiness lies with the man is not that much true.*
*Nice posting.*
*Regards.*

*Somnath Banerjee in reply to Prakash Chavan*
*Man has so many roles to perform, there is mask for each one.*
*happiness is state of bliss unaffected by ambient condition*
*a choice has been made, he has to enjoy pain and pleasure associated with it. he is happy.*

*Umesh Hannikeri*
*Jai Sairam!! Thanks for sharing this wonderful thoughts! This is really nice piece of information. Thought provoking.*

*Somnath Banerjee in reply to Umesh Hannikeri*
*Get Ramji in your conscience and your choice shall be right.*
*Mandar K*
*Gud*

*Somnath Banerjee in reply to Mandar K*
*Your choice, thanks*

## 67. MONKEY KING

*Narsimha Saraswati*
*Thus, according to Napoleon -*
*If a person is intelligent and lazy he shall go to the top*
*Is this the best class of person?*

*Somnath Banerjee in reply to Narsimha Saraswati*
*They make dream come true.*

*Bipin Chandra*
*Spirituality is personal communion with the inner Reality, religion simply helps in preparing for it thanks.*

**Somnath Banerjee in reply to Bipin Chandra**
*Very true*

**Rutvij Kothari**
*Very well said. In life we need to find correct person to be reliable and you can trust him.. Agree with the point you made about Ego. In life Confidence and Attitude also play huge role.. Because thing which are done with confidence get 99% success ration and with positive attitude you can solve out any hurdles.. That's how life is placed... You can do it.. You just need to lighten your inner soul..*
*But very good message given.. Awesome words.. :)*

**Somnath Banerjee in reply to Rutvij Kothari**
*What do you think about people deeply religious but no spirituality*

**Rutvij Kothari in reply to Somnath Banerjee**
*But young generation won't think deeply religious.. Telling it from my personal experience... :)*

**Somnath Banerjee in reply to Rutvij Kothari**
*Three types of people can be visualized*
*1, Religious no spirituality 40%*
*2. spiritual with no religion 10%*
*3. No religion and no spirituality 50%*

**Madhusudan Attaluri**
*SomanathJi, Namasthe.*
*I thought that designate king was Rahul Gandhi. Disappointed.*

**Somnath Banerjee in reply to Madhusudan Attalur...**
*In every organisation there people holding responsible post without accountability.*
*The cap may fit Rahul. how do you like the story. religion without spirituality.*

**Madhusudan Attaluri in reply to Somnath Banerjee**
*Rituals mean Pooja (worship). This is one of the definite ways of Bhakti. King Ambarish does only Pooja of Vishnu. His devotion is so pure that he had sought nothing from The Lord. The Lord Himself had come to the rescue of Ambarish when he was in life threat. And He Himself appeared before Ambarish and handed over Sudarshan Chakra to him for preserving and worship.*

*Observance of Rituals, in fact, requires lot of commitment (shraddha). In Shraddha the mind deeply dips in the thinking of God. So,my views slightly differ.*

**Somnath Banerjee in reply to Madhusudan Attalur...**
*When a sapling is small it needs protection from herbivorous elements, however when it becomes a tree, no protection is needed, similarly after enlightenment, rituals become redundant.*
*s the fruit you bear for upward mobility*

## 69. PEACE AND HARMONY REIGN IN UNISON

**Monsoon God**
*Somnath ji,*
*Living in Peace and Harmony is not an easy thing to do. From the moment we are conceived, we are bombarded with obstacles that try to hinder us from evolving in an environment of Peace and Harmony. I don't have to point out all the things of this world and environment that are creating chaos of spirit, mind and body. We are all experiencing the same things. However, the difference is the way we deal with all things of life. To live in Peace and Harmony in this existence, we must first learn to live in Peace and Harmony with ourselves. So how do we re-establish balance? By making manifest a world of Peace in our individual lives and environment. How do we do that? By creating it.*

**Somnath Banerjee in reply to Monsoon God**
*Living in Peace and Harmony is not an easy thing to do.' very true. we are considering a state of a person who has transcended above body and mind*

*All thoughts of confrontation dissipated, such a person shall gain peace and harmony*

**Sunita Gupta**
*Great thoughtful message --delivered in few slides only. ......get over body consciousness !*

**Somnath Banerjee in reply to Sunita Gupta**
*Thanks only few people understand it*

*Sunita Gupta in reply to Somnath Banerjee*
*Those few may not be the part of the rat race.*

*Somnath Banerjee in reply to Sunita Gupta*
*How true. they forget you may win all the rat race you are still a rat*

*Meera Panigrahi*
*Nice slide show. Where there is peace there is harmony.*

*Somnath Banerjee in reply to Meera Panigrahi*
*Peace can be the result of both happiness and sadness. However harmony means to be calm due to happiness, love and friendship. Harmony means team work peace is personal, harmony means sharing*

## 70. PERCEIVED TRAITS AND POSSIBLE OUTCOMES

*Pavan Raina*
*Beautiful Somanath jee: Rich experience is earned and what an satisfying outcome can be achieved but difficult to express and induct in others. Nice one need to keep expanding his own consciousness and then every thing sets itself by the Divine help.*

*Somnath Banerjee in reply to Pavan Raina*
*These traits are the weapons bestowed on goddess Durga, Divine traits, the possible outcome is only one of them, you may ponder on the outcome there is multiple choice. your survival may be at stake.*

*Abc Narayan*
*Good traits and good outcomes.*

*Somnath Banerjee in reply to Abc Narayan*
*These traits are the weapons bestowed on goddess Durga, the possible outcome is only one of them, you may ponder on the outcome --best wishes*

## 71. RADHA - PRINCESS OF BEAUTY AND GRACE

*Bipin Chandra Padhy*
*Http://www.speakingtree.in/public/spiritual-blogs/ seekers/ science-of-spirituality/the-glorious-life- and-message-of- sukadeva,kindly bless sir.*

**Somnath Banerjee in reply to Bipin Chandra Padh...**
*Krishna Leela as mind conjure bring peace in body and mind.*
*om tat sat*

**Bipin Chandra Padhy in reply to Somnath Banerjee**
*Thanks sir.*

**Shekhar Ray**
*Radhe Radhe :-) :-) :-)*

**Somnath Banerjee in reply to Shekhar Ray**
*Hare Krishna.... radha madhav they are inseparable and most probably same soul in two bodies.*

**Shekhar Ray in reply to Somnath Banerjee**
*In reality Soul is one and only one. ........Paramatma. Although it express through so many bodies as Jivatma.*

**Somnath Banerjee in reply to Shekhar Ray**
*Lord Krishna's play not easy to explain. Krishna projected female propensities as Radha*

**Subodh Patnaik**
*Radha has beauty which is incomparable.UR slide show is fantastic.U should go through the GITAGOVINDAM OF POET JAYDEV.*

**Somnath Banerjee in reply to Subodh Patnaik**
*Krishna was < twelve years old. Jaydev is imagining transformation of love in physical domain with spiritual domain.*
*I have projected that attributes of Radha are no different from Krishna,*

**Subodh Patnaik in reply to Somnath Banerjee**
*Thank u.*

**Somnath Banerjee in reply to Subodh Patnaik**
*Welcome*

**Shri Dattaswami**
*Devotion*

*The relationship of the devotee with the Lord is called devotion. Devotion is love for he Lord. Love is proved by service or seva. Claims of love without service are fraudulent. Praying, meditation, intellectual discussions, words, feelings or singing hymns does not substantiate devotion. If a husband loves his wife then he must serve her when she is ill. If he just sits by her side with his eyes closed or meditates upon her or chants her name aloud, while refusing to practically serve her by giving her medicines, food and drink, then he is only making a show of love; he does not really love her. The one who really loves her will serve her.*

*The Lord is pleased only with total devotion. The Gita says "eka bhakti? visi?yate". He wants the devotee to love Him alone; not anyone or anything else. Nobody or nothing should be equal to Him. He will make the devotee reach this stage of devotion. This is the essence of all the datta parik?a or the tests of the Lord. The devotee will be tested severely till he breaks all bonds with everyone and everything in the world, till only the bond with the Lord remains. The Lord does not compromise in this aspect. He will not tolerate even a drop of the devotee's attachment to anything or anyone in the world.*

*Lord Krishna tested Radha very severely.*

*She was His beloved in vrndavanam. When the Lord left vrndavanam he left her behind. Not only that but He even married other women. He offered protection to sixteen thousand women. He never returned to vrndavanam to Radha. He never inquired about her. He never even saw her face again. Such was the severity of His test. His intention was to see if Radha would get jealous. The weakness of a woman is her lover. No woman can tolerate any other women around her lover. Radha, who was the Lord's beloved, for many years in vrndavanam had all the reason to get jealous of the wives of Lord Krishna. Yet her love was pure. It was free of expectation. She never once gave in to jealousy. She was ever full of love for Him. She would constantly imagine herself falling at the feet of the Lord. She died pining for Him. The Lord was extremely pleased with her and gave her his eternal companionship in the uppermost world.*

*The Lord tested Hanuman in the aspect of egotism. He gave Hanuman ample opportunity to develop egotism. Lord Rama never displayed any special powers to prove that He was the Lord. Hanuman himself had a lot of super powers and had to use them more than Lord Rama. The Lord also made sure that Hanuman was compelled to use those powers to save Him. He made Hanuman save Lakshmana's life by lifting the dro?agiri mountain in order to obtain the life saving sañjivani herb. When Lord Rama and Lakshmana, both were knocked unconscious by the powerful demon, indrajit, Hanuman had to fly to the heavens and bring garu?a the Divine Eagle, in order to save them. Thus the Lord made it appear that it was Hanuman, who was never incapacitated in the war while the Lord Himself was. It was Hanuman who had to rescue the Lord. It was Hanuman who displayed super powers and not the Lord. It would appear to a common observer that Hanuman was the Lord and not Lord Rama. However Hanuman's devotion was sublime. He did not fall pray to egotism. He understood fully well that Lord Rama was the Lord and that He was only testing him. He therefore said "daso'ha? kosalendrasya; "I am the servant of the Lord."*

### Somnath Banerjee in reply to Shri Dattaswami
*My blog is not on devotion but on Radha princess of beauty and grace,*

### Shri Dattaswami
*The psychology of the people is to get attraction towards the things, which are far and to get detached from the things, which are very close. Infact, this is the general psychology of souls and even angels are not exceptional as said in Veda 'Paroksha Priya ivahi devah pratyaksha dvishah...', which means that even angels like any item, which is far and dislike any item present before the eyes. This is the reason for God keeping us in close association with worldly atmosphere and to keep Himself far from us. Whatever God does is always meaningful and we criticize God without understanding Him in depth.*

*You should always be closely associated with the items from which you want detachment. You should always keep yourself far from the items on which you like to maintain your attraction. When the item existing away from you becomes closely associated, your attraction towards it starts diminishing. This is the reason for the repulsion towards the contemporary human incarnation, which exists before your eyes. Similarly, the reason for attraction to past human incarnations and the energetic incarnations of God related to the upper world is that these forms are not before your eyes.*

*One day Radha came to Dwaraka from Brindavanam and Rukmini gave her hot milk. Rukmini also was taking the same hot milk every day but on that day Krishna became red due to heat. On enquiry Krishna told that since He is in the heart of Radha, His body became red due to the hot milk taken by Radha. Then Rukmini asked the Lord for not seeing the same effect every day since she was also taking the same hot milk. The Lord told that since He is in the heart of Radha only, the effect was seen. Rukmini asked the reason for the difference between her and Radha. The Lord told that since Rukmini is staying very close to Him, her devotion was not as strong as that of Radha, who was staying in Brindavanam far from Him. This story shows that close association always leads to the negligence.*

**Somnath Banerjee in reply to Shri Dattaswami**
*Radha and Krishna are not different. lord Shiva is Ardhanariswar. Every person has male and female attributes associated. In case of Radha and Krishna they are depicted*

**Sham Lal Mehta**
*In our legends Radha--the divine consort of Lord Krishna--stands for everything fine that can be attributed to a female i.e. grace, love, beauty, softness and sweetness. And she is endowed with the rare fortune, the love and affection of Lord Krishna. Who on the earth can be luckier than her.*

**Somnath Banerjee in reply to Sham Lal Mehta**
*I may stand corrected, RUKMANIi is the divine consort of Lord Krishna,*
*Radha is the female complement of Lord Krishna,*
*So I have highlighted all the attributes of Lord Krishna to Radha.*
*Radhe Radhe*

**Sham Lal Mehta in reply to Somnath Banerjee**
*Yes, Mr. Banerjee, you are right. Rukmini being legally wedded wife is the divine consort. Radha, on the other hand, is the soul mate, one with lord--there being no DVAITA BHAVA, as Lord Krishna himself has shown.*
*My regards.*

*Somnath Banerjee in reply to Sham Lal Mehta*
*With devotion and surrender we also can be soul mate of Lord Krishna om tat sat*

## 72. RAINY DAY ANTS TAUGHT ME

*Shekhar Ray*
ফুল সে হাসিতে হাসিতে ঝরে, জ্যোছনা হাসিয়া মিলায়ে যায়,
হাসিতে হাসিতে আলোক সাগরে আকাশের ও তারা তেয়াগে তায়।

*Flower drops down smilingly, Moonlight dims off within its smile,*
*The sky renounces its Stars in the ocean of light with a smile.*

*Somnath Banerjee in reply to Shekhar Ray*
*Your beautiful quote is as per cycle of nature.*
*I found behavior of ant against the survival instinct, dominant in all animals.*
*Ants line up for metamorphosis knowing fully well that they shall perish next day.*
*Self scarifies for continuity of species.*

*Shekhar Ray in reply to Somnath Banerjee*
*Possibly there are some bird called Finix having similar nature.*

*Somnath Banerjee in reply to Shekhar Ray*
*Every five hundred years Phoenix or Finix, when it begins to feel weak and old, it flies west to the mountain. There it builds a fragrant nest on top of a palm tree, and there the sun once again burns it to ashes. But each time, the Phoenix rises up from those ashes, fresh and new and young again.*

*Suman Bala*
*You have beautifully correlated the intelligence of ants with human psyche.*
*I too had posted a blog sometimes back on the lessons that we can learn from this small yet very intelligent creature.*

*Somnath Banerjee in reply to Suman Bala*
*Appreciating the nature we wonder, then ponder.*
*in spite of the fact that we try to be immune from nature*
*in the end we surrender to it.*
**Sangameswaran Nura**...*Very beautiful and inspirational. Thanks a lot.*

*Somnath Banerjee in reply to Sangameswaran Nura...*
Om tat sat

## 73. SALVATION FROM SIN

*Narsimha Saraswati*
*Very true!*

*All actions to fulfill insatiable desires for worldly pleasures of senses takes us away from spirituality.*

*Any such deed which effects repeated birth and death is sin, the deed that prompts one towards God and begets the ultimate repose is piety.*

*Getting rid of desires will result in getting rid of anger, greed, pride or ego, jealousy and attachment.*

**Somnath Banerjee in reply to Narsimha Saraswati**
*Interaction of senses with sense objects create attachment, from attachment springs desire, so your suggestion to get rid of desire shall entail getting rid of senses or sense objects which is not possible.*

*For preserving Immortality of life repeated birth and death is essential. The activities that lead to cycle of birth and death cannot be sin.*

*Narsimha Saraswati in reply to Somnath Banerjee*
*Namaskaar Somnath Ji!*

*When one knows that his true inner self is Aatma and not the body, 5 senses, mind, memory, intelligence and ego then it is possible to take away these away from their objects. 5 senses are more powerful than body. Mind is more powerful than 5 senses. Intelligence is more powerful than mind. Aatma is more powerful than intelligence With practice (Abhyaas) it is possible to take body, 5 senses, mind, memory, intelligence and ego away from their objects. One can not force it. Also one can not copy others. It has to come naturally with practice. With practice gradually Nivrutti from Vishay Bhog can be attained. When one focuses all energies to realize true nature of Aatma which is Paramaatma then all is possible. When one has this higher goal to realize true nature of self then all other things become less important.*

*For any human being the highest goal is to realize its true nature of Aatma which is Paramaatma. If desires and actions to fulfill those desires are causing the repeating cycle of birth and death then one is leading Aatma on the path of descent. Leading ones Aatma on this path of descent is the sin.*

**Somnath Banerjee in reply to Narsimha Saraswati**
*'When one focuses all energies to realize true nature of Aatma which is Paramaatma then all is possible.'*
*very true.*
*please highlight which all energies are involved.*
*Vivekananda states you have to focus strength of Atma.*
*other energy is sexual energy.*
*Neural network is statistically multiplexed system*

**Gopi Dhondare**
*User blocked by admin*

**Somnath Banerjee in reply to Gopi Dhondare**
*Thanks*

**Gopi Dhondare in reply to Somnath Banerjee**
*User blocked by admin*

**Somnath Banerjee in reply to Gopi Dhondare**
*My next blog commentryy on i am god....*

**Shekhar Ray**
*In reality there is neither sin/ Paap nor Punya. ...... both are just concept exist in human mind and body-mind suffers or enjoys its consequences. ..... real salvation is just annihilation of the concept of Paap-Punya in individual mind.*

**Somnath Banerjee in reply to Shekhar Ray**
*You have brought out the gist of the blog.*
*'real salvation is just annihilation of the concept of Paap-Punya in individual mind. '*
*The methodology has been highlighted in the blog*

**Prakash Bagga in reply to Shekhar Ray**

*PAAP is reference for any evil thought particularly harming other human beings or other beingss or even any creation of the creator.. Thus the PAAP one can commit knowingly or unknowingly too.*

*In SGGS ji there is a clear message in this context as "NUR ACHET PAAP TE DUR RE:*

*Means..Human Being,You should fear even from unknowing evil thought*

**Somnath Banerjee in reply to Prakash Bagga**

*Like Jesus brought out that every person commit sin. There is nothing to fear from sin.*

*You can always get salvation, it helps in propagation of a religion. Thoughts shall be generated it is your intellect to decide and EGO to veto.*

**Tanweer Ahmad**

7

*Salvation*

*Man having arrived in this house of darkness cannot attain salvation unless, being himself honored by the converse of God, or keeping company with someone who is the recipient of sure revelation and who has witnessed clear signs, he arrives at the certain knowledge that he has a God Who is Powerful, Benevolent and Merciful, and that Islam which is his faith is in fact true and the Judgment Day and heaven and hell are realities. As a matter of tradition all Muslims believe in the existence of God and in the truth of the Holy Prophet, but this faith has no sure foundation. Through such weak faith it is not possible to be deeply affected and to hate sin {Nazulul Masih ( Qadian, Ziaul Islam Press 1909) Now prited in Ruhani Khazain (London, 1984) vol. 18, p. I07-108}.*

*The true meaning of salvation*

*It is a pity that most people are unaware of the true meaning of salvation. According to the Christians, salvation means deliverance from the punishment of sin. This is not the true meaning of salvation. It is possible that a person may not commit adultery or theft, or bear false witness, or kill anyone, or commit any other sin so far as he knows, and yet be unacquainted with salvation, for salvation means the achievement of that eternal prosperity for which human nature hungers and thirsts. It is achieved only through the personal love of God after His full understanding and the establishment of a perfect relationship with Him and its condition is that love should surge up on both sides....*

*For a seeker after truth the only question is how to achieve true prosperity which should be the means of eternal joy and happiness. The sign of a true religion is that it should carry one to that prosperity. Through the guidance of the Holy Quran we learn that that eternal prosperity is found in the true understanding of God Almighty and His holy and perfect and personal love, and in perfect faith which should create a lover's restlessness in the heart. These are a few words and yet it would take a volume to set forth an exposition of them {Chashmai Masihi (Qadian, Magazine Press, 1906), Now published in Ruhani Khazain (London, 1984) vol.20, p. 32-34}.*

*What the Holy Quran has said in this context amounts to this: O My servants, do not despair of Me. I am Merciful and Benevolent and cover up sins and forgive them and am more Merciful towards you than anyone else. No one will have mercy on you as I have. Love me more than you love your fathers for I am greater in love than they are. If you come to me I shall forgive all your sins and if you repent, I shall accept your repentance. If you advance towards me slowly, I shall run to you. He who seeks Me shall find Me and He who turns to Me shall find My door open. I forgive the sins of a penitent even if they are more than the mountains. My mercy upon you is great and my wrath is little because you are My creatures. I have created you and therefore My mercy comprises all of you {Chashmai Ma'arafat ( Qadian, Anwar Ahmadiyyah Press, 1908) Now published in Ruhani Khazain (London, 1984) vol. 23., p. 48}.*

### Somnath Banerjee in reply to Tanweer Ahmad

*"This faith has no sure foundation. "the faith has strong foundation of Peace & universal brotherhood.*

*Methodology provided for eradication of Lust, & greed which are most common cause for sin.*

*"salvation means the achievement of that eternal prosperity for which human nature hungers and thirsts."*

*When life is limited how salvation can mean eternal prosperity.*
*lastly God accepts that you will sin and he will forgive, so continue*
*with the sins, f it becomes hard to bear ask for Gods forgiveness,*
*ones he forgives aagain continue with your sins as Salvation is*
*Guarenteed*

## 74. SMILE PLEASE

**Arijit Sarkar**
*Laughing is good for heakth*
*Reply*

**Somnath Banerjee in reply to Arijit Sarkar**
*There is laughter therapy, but smiling is not laughing.*

**Shekhar Ray**
*:-))))))))))))))))*

**Somnath Banerjee in reply to Shekhar Ray**
*Seeing play of nature- you smile mindfully*

**Hitesh Jain**
*Smile is the only language understood by even newly born baby.*

**Somnath Banerjee in reply to Hitesh Jain**
*True, but dont underestimate a child- he understands much more*
*than you think*

## 75. SUCCESS PRINCIPLES IN PHYSICAL AND SPIRITUAL DOMAIN ARE SAME

**Sksg**
*Well said !!*

**Somnath Banerjee in reply to Sksg**
*Thanks*

**Manmohan Kumar**
*That's why they say चलती का नाम गाढ़ी = nothing succeeds like*
*success ||*

**Somnath Banerjee in reply to Manmohan Kumar**
*Nothing succeeds like success || '*

*My aim was to show that path to success is same though the domain change from Material to spiritual.*

## 77. YARDSTICK IS VARIABLE

**Meera Panigrahi**
*We all have different yardsticks to measure good and bad. We must learn to apply this stick to our own selves to see where we stand in the scheme of values.*

**Somnath Banerjee in reply to Meera Panigrahi**
*This yardstick is held very secret*
*As emotional state depends on it*
*Yet this yardstick compels us*
*To measure against actual state*
*Sometime we are left wanting*
*Sometime we are overwhelmed by it.*
*your yardstick shall change when you see where you stand*

**Col Gurnam Singh**
*My yardstick changes as my experience grows and also as I forget those experiences that have faded to a mere vapor trail in the travails of life.*

**Sunita Gupta in reply to Col Gurnam Singh**
*That is wonderful Col Gurnam ji. ....change is law of nature and we need to change our self as we grow both in age, maturity and wisdom......while learning in the school called life. .....thanx !*

**Somnath Banerjee in reply to Sunita Gupta**
*Like todays comfort becomes garbage and we have to throw it out*

**Sunita Gupta in reply to Somnath Banerjee**
*Waqt and kal. ..all depends on time and age and of course greed factor !*

**Somnath Banerjee in reply to Sunita Gupta**
*True*

**Sunita Gupta in reply to Somnath Banerjee**
*Regards nd good night !!*

**Somnath Banerjee in reply to Sunita Gupta**
*Same to you,*

**Somnath Banerjee in reply to Col Gurnam Singh**
*Discipline and security is provided by yardstick, compromising them may be detrimental to your spiritual upliftment*

**Col Gurnam Singh in reply to Somnath Banerjee**
*You are right!*

**Somnath Banerjee in reply to Col Gurnam Singh**
*Welcome*

**Sunita Gupta in reply to Somnath Banerjee**
*So true !*

**Somnath Banerjee in reply to Sunita Gupta**
*Thanks*

**Sunita Gupta**
*Well we come down accumulate ; then we go empty handed ; every religion stresses upon the need to play a fair play while being on this pilgrimage over here. ... even if we loose in the eyes of world how does it matter until i can face myself, my inner self with courage and conviction. ..no failure matters to me. ...ultimately all is between me and my god*

**Somnath Banerjee in reply to Sunita Gupta**
*Religions are yardsticks which may modify your yardstick as per your propensities.*
*Your wisdom is not accepted by rest of the world, well it does not matter*

**Sunita Gupta in reply to Somnath Banerjee**
*Let me carve my own path at least now. ...i will now love to walk on my own path !*

**Somnath Banerjee in reply to Sunita Gupta**
*Yes you are god of your world*

**Sunita Gupta**
*Everybody has a yardstick*
*Measuring others by it*
*wonderful opening lines !*

**Somnath Banerjee in reply to Sunita Gupta**
*You loose yardstick when you have equamity. or it gets minimized.*

**Sunita Gupta in reply to Somnath Banerjee**
*So true. ..in the light of the soul !!*

**Somnath Banerjee in reply to Sunita Gupta**
*Your voice of conscience is continually providing with yardstick, yet you make your own*

**Sunita Gupta in reply to Somnath Banerjee**
*Sometimes yes, mind may take over but i revert back very soon !*
*Somnath Banerjee in reply to Sunita Gupta*
*Showing veto power of ego.*

**Sunita Gupta in reply to Somnath Banerjee**
*Yes, but depends how much we let it take over.*

**Somnath Banerjee in reply to Sunita Gupta**
*Clashing with your yardstick*

**Sunita Gupta in reply to Somnath Banerjee**
*No ! never !*

**Somnath Banerjee in reply to Sunita Gupta**
*With chalta hai attitude of youth today*
*can you sum up your yardstick*

**Sunita Gupta in reply to Somnath Banerjee**
*Yes, but depends how much you get carried away by mind.*

**Somnath Banerjee in reply to Sunita Gupta**
*Get carried away it will give peace and happiness*

**Sunita Gupta in reply to Somnath Banerjee**
*It may give momentary happiness but never lasting peace & happiness !!*

**Somnath Banerjee in reply to Sunita Gupta**
*Mind left to itself reaches bliss (transcendental Meditation)*

**Sunita Gupta in reply to Somnath Banerjee**
*If find time plz share. ....http://www.speakingtree.in/public/ spiritual-b logs/seekers/science-of-spirituality/who-will-solv e-the-mystery-of-mind*

**Somnath Banerjee in reply to Sunita Gupta**
*Ok*

## 78. CREATE YOUR SMALL WORLD

**Sham Lal Mehta**
*Our scriptures say--nothing goes with you in next life except your karmas. Thus, good karmas are the only best investment that one can make.*

**Somnath Banerjee in reply to Sham Lal Mehta**
*Very true, as per scripture you are soul which takes on different bodies, even during one life all your body cells are changed in seven years, you reap the fruit of investment in this life only, my submission inthe blog is that you are your world by yourself*

**Zaki Akhter**
*Nice. ..but needs some rectification...*

**Somnath Banerjee in reply to Zaki Akhter**
*Please do rectify, and forward your views*

**Shekhar Ray**
*Last slide: Harvest the crops at proper time ! But a spiritual person sows seeds not to reap the fruit himself but for all.*

**Somnath Banerjee in reply to Shekhar Ray**
*In the physical domain fruit of investment is well known. In the spiritual domain you are not different from others
leading to fearlessness and cheerfulness*

**Sandesh Saboo**
*User blocked by admin*

**Book Nook**
*Great slideshow...only wish there were more such slides with very meaningful quotes...Thank You!*

**Somnath Banerjee in reply to Book Nook**
*Let us see whether i can live up to your expectation.thanks*

**Shekhar Ray**
*The symbol in first slide represents the existence of all opposites in human beings.*

**Somnath Banerjee in reply to Shekhar Ray**
*The attributes of soul has both divine and demoniacal qualities ch16 Gita.*

**Lalit Mohan**
*You are free by nature, so what will you achieve by forcing the mind? Jai Jagdambey*

**Somnath Banerjee in reply to Lalit Mohan**
*Man is born free but in chain. chains of family, society, nation etc, i submit that your mind is the world you perceive*
*You are to tap the knowledge. how?*
*Try by listening to voice of conscience. om tat sat*

**Subash Dash**
*Great. drives in right direction is always safe. do you agree with it ?.*

**Somnath Banerjee in reply to Subash Dash**
*Choice is yours. there is no right or wrong direction only pain and pleasure are different. final outcome is same.*
*do you agree.*

**Bipin Chandra Padhy**
*It is a question of depending upon our higher or lower mind. greatness lies in conquering lower mind by higher min d and then transcending the higher mind.Thanks for your nice sharing.sir.*

**Somnath Banerjee in reply to Bipin Chandra Padh...**
*There is no higher or lower mind. mind conjure your world by spatial disposition and time integration. transcending the mind, you are god or dog.*
*best of luck*

**Bipin Chandra Padhy in reply to Somnath Banerjee**
*In meditation and deep silence lies the answer! thanks.*

**Somnath Banerjee in reply to Bipin Chandra Padh...**
*You can get answer once you have identified the question. GI=GO*

**Sunita Gupta**
*Great thoughts, so one has to decide and then be happy with that or decide to have a balanced life.*

**Somnath Banerjee in reply to Sunita Gupta**
*Choice is yours,as long as you are greated with smile with eyes lighting up!*

**Sunita Gupta in reply to Somnath Banerjee**
*So what even at times life does not smile at you ---you smile back at life and make it to smile back at you by being a winner !*

**Somnath Banerjee in reply to Sunita Gupta**
*That is the spirit.*
*human life means a winner in evolutionary race,*
*keep the winning habit with full grace.*

**Sunita Gupta in reply to Somnath Banerjee**
*Thanks nd regards. .with a blessed day ahead.*

# INDEX ALPHABETICAL

## ABOUT THE AUTHOR

Dr Banerjee was educated at St Philomena's convent, Pune university and IIT Delhi. He retired as Colonel in Indian army and was awarded Commendation card for innovations in the field of Telecommunication. He served Qatar Telecommunication as Network Architecture Specialist and is a director of an Engineering college.

His writing is purely based on self experience. He wants to share his perception so that we can become good human beings. His work is original, some of poetries were published by Inter national Poetry. com and had also received Editor choice award in 2007.

Dr Somnath Banerjee does not accept any theism without analysis and inquiry. He has hands on knowledge in Christianity being schooled in convent, he was initiated into Hinduism at tender age with thread ceremony. After completing doctorate in physics from Pune university joined army he was posted to Arunachal pradesh where he developed fair taste in Buddhism. He served Qatar telecom for four years he developed affinity for Islam.

Dr S S Banerjee is an academician and a high-tech army officer. He was selected Network Architecture Specialist by Qatar Telecom. After returning to India, served Amity University as Professor (Telecom), Director of ABES Institute of Technology at Ghaziabad, GITM (Gurgaon), SIEM (Mathura). Apart from technical papers he has written two books Introspection & Results of Consciousness.

**For further correspond**
**Dr S S Banerjee**
**C20 Manas Apartment**
**Mayur Vihar Phase 1**
**Delhi 110091**
**Email ssb1950@yahoo.com,** drssbanerjee@gmail.com

www.ingramcontent.com/pod-product-compliance
Lightning Source LLC
Chambersburg PA
CBHW031429270326
41930CB00007B/627